Famous Hollywood Locations

Famous Hollywood Locations

McFarland Classics

Anderson. *Science Fiction Films of the Seventies*
Archer. *Willis O'Brien*
Benson. *Vintage Science Fiction Films, 1896–1949*
Bernardoni. *The New Hollywood*
Broughton. *Producers on Producing*
Byrge & Miller. *The Screwball Comedy Films*
Chesher. *"The End": Closing Lines...*
Cline. *In the Nick of Time*
Cline. *Serials-ly Speaking*
Darby & Du Bois. *American Film Music*
Derry. *The Suspense Thriller*
Douglas. *The Early Days of Radio Broadcasting*
Drew. *D.W. Griffith's* Intolerance
Ellrod. *Hollywood Greats of the Golden Years*
Erickson. *Religious Radio and Television in the U.S., 1921–1991*
Erickson. *Syndicated Television*
Frasier. *Russ Meyer—The Life and Films*
Fury. *Kings of the Jungle*
Galbraith. *Motor City Marquees*
Harris. *Children's Live-Action Musical Films*
Harris. *Film and Television Composers*
Hayes. *The Republic Chapterplays*
Hayes. *3-D Movies*
Hayes. *Trick Cinematography*
Hill. *Raymond Burr*
Hogan. *Dark Romance*
Holland. *B Western Actors Encyclopedia*
Horner. *Bad at the Bijou*
Jarlett. *Robert Ryan*
Kinnard. *Horror in Silent Films*

Langman & Gold. *Comedy Quotes from the Movies*
Levine. *The 247 Best Movie Scenes in Film History*
McGee. *Beyond Ballyhoo*
McGee. *The Rock & Roll Movie Encyclopedia of the 1950s*
McGee. *Roger Corman*
McGhee. *John Wayne*
Mank. *Hollywood Cauldron: Thirteen Horror Films*
Martin. *The Allied Artists Checklist*
Nollen. *The Boys: ...Laurel and Hardy*
Nowlan. *Cinema Sequels and Remakes, 1903–1987*
Okuda. *The Monogram Checklist*
Okuda & Watz. *The Columbia Comedy Shorts*
Parish. *Prison Pictures from Hollywood*
Pitts. *Western Movies*
Quarles. *Down and Dirty: Hollywood's Exploitation Filmmakers*
Selby. *Dark City: The Film Noir*
Sigoloff. *The Films of the Seventies*
Slide. *Nitrate Won't Wait*
Smith. *Famous Hollywood Locations*
Sturcken. *Live Television*
Tropp. *Images of Fear*
Tuska. *The Vanishing Legion: ...Mascot Pictures*
Von Gunden. *Alec Guinness*
Von Gunden. *Flights of Fancy*
Warren. *Keep Watching the Skies!*
Watson. *Television Horror Movie Hosts*
Watz. *Wheeler & Woolsey*
Weaver. *Poverty Row HORRORS!*
Weaver. *Return of the B Science Fiction and Horror Heroes*
West. *Television Westerns*

Famous Hollywood Locations

*Descriptions and Photographs
of 382 Sites Involving 289 Films
and 105 Television Series*

by
LEON SMITH

McFarland
Classics

McFarland & Company, Inc., Publishers
Jefferson, North Carolina, and London

Leon Smith is also the author of
Movie and Television Locations (McFarland, 2000)

The present work is a reprint of the library bound edition of Famous
Hollywood Locations: Descriptions and Photographs of 382 Sites
Involving 289 Films and 105 Television Series, *first published in
1993.* **McFarland Classics** *is an imprint of McFarland & Company,
Inc., Publishers, Jefferson, North Carolina, who also published the
original edition.*

Library of Congress Cataloguing-in-Publication Data

Smith, Leon.
    Famous Hollywood locations : descriptions and photographs of 382
sites involving 289 films and 105 television series / by Leon Smith.
        p.   cm.
    Includes index.
    ISBN 0-7864-1116-3 (softcover : 50# alkaline paper) ∞
    1. Motion picture locations—California—Los Angeles Region—
Guidebooks.   2. Television program locations—California—Los
Angeles Region—Guidebooks.   3. Los Angeles Region (Calif.)—
Guidebooks.   I. Title.
PN1995.67.L67S64   2001   791.43'025'79494—dc20   92-56697

British Library cataloguing data are available

On the cover: A shot from the 1975 film *The Day of the Locust* (Photofest)

Manufactured in the United States of America

McFarland & Company, Inc., Publishers
    Box 611, Jefferson, North Carolina 28640
    www.mcfarlandpub.com

To the Hollywood Motion Picture
and Television Industry

ACKNOWLEDGMENTS

My deep appreciation to: the Academy of Motion Picture Arts and Sciences (Robert Cushman), KCET Public Television (Connie Babilonia), the Los Angeles City Motion Picture Coordinating Office (Dirk Beving), Lorimar Telepictures Corporation (Jerry Osnower), The Newhall Land & Farming Company (Lou Rion and Dawn), Olive View Medical Center (Carolyn Rhee); and Russell Bolton, Bob Bonday, John Castillo, Michael Hawks, Rich Rosenberg, Georgia Smith, Kathryn Smith, Leon Smith, Jr., Jim Walters, and Stephen A. Wichrowski, Jr.

CONTENTS

PREFACE

The title of this book refers to the physical locations in and near the city of Los Angeles and the country of Mexico used to film segments of motion pictures and television series. All locations listed in this publication have been identified through review of films, videotapes, still photographs taken at the time of filming and printed matter relating to the motion picture and television series production. To confirm the authenticity of each site, I have personally visited all locations included in this book. The research for this book encompassed vast stretches of Los Angeles city and county, from the far reaches of the San Fernando Valley to the southern section of the city, and from the Pacific Ocean to East Los Angeles. Some of the material in this book has previously appeared in four other books written by this author (*A Guide to Laurel and Hardy Movie Locations* and *Following the Comedy Trail*, published by G.J. Enterprises in 1982 and 1984 respectively, and *Following the Comedy Trail: A Compilation* and *Hollywood Goes on Location*, both published by Pomegranate Press in 1988).

If you visit these locations, please remember that most of the residences are occupied and, of course, are private and that many of the commercial properties restrict entry without express permission. So please use discretion and courtesy. Do not trespass on private property or disturb the privacy of any person.

Also keep in mind that many locations are close to other locations. So to avoid backtracking, review the locations before a visit. For example, in downtown Los Angeles two *War of the Worlds* sites are just across the street from an *L.A. Law* site; the theater seen in *La Bamba* is close to the Carnation Building (the lobby of the *Daily Planet* from *The Adventures of Superman* television series) which, in turn, is very close to "ground zero" seen in *Miracle Mile;* the house seen in television's *Leave It to Beaver* is only a few blocks from the house seen in Laurel and Hardy's 1927 classic comedy *Love 'Em and Weep;* the Culver City site of *Barfly* is but across the street from a location seen in *A Nightmare on Elm Street 5: The Dream Child.*

Additionally, many films begin at one location and end at another. Occasionally other locations are used in between. In such instances, the location first seen in the film will be the primary film location, with additional film

The author, at the Hollywood Studio Museum at the office of Cecil B. DeMille.

locations listed in the narrative portion and cross-referenced in the appropriate sections of this book.

Take your time and plan your visit well. To provide as much assistance as I can, especially to visitors from out of the city of Los Angeles or the state of California—or the United States for that matter—I've grouped the sites geographically, beginning with the city of Los Angeles, followed by Hollywood, with the remaining communities listed in alphabetical order.

The Thomas Brothers Map references listed throughout this text refer to coordinates in the current edition of the Thomas Brothers Guide, Los Angeles County Street Atlas and Directory, which is on sale at most Los Angeles stationery shops and bookstores, or can be ordered by mail from Thomas Brothers Maps and Books, 603 West Seventh Street, Los Angeles, CA 90017.

Note: After 76 years, Thomas Brothers redesigned their Los Angeles map books. The revisions begin with the 1992 edition and are included in the present work, as are page numbers and grids from previous Thomas Brothers map books for convenient reference.

For the serious film buff, I have included a synopsis of each film, with applicable Academy Award nominations and Oscar winners. In addition, a comprehensive index containing names, places, monuments, landmarks, studios, films and television series is found at the back of the book.

Leon Smith

INTRODUCTION

The Hollywood section of Los Angeles is much more than a community in which was spawned the motion picture and television industry as we know it today. It is a gigantic magnet that perpetually draws those seeking fame and fortune in films and those who simply want to pay a visit and see where it all happened and is happening today.

At this time, however, Hollywood retains few of the film studios that propelled a fledgling industry into a prominence unparalleled in world history, Paramount Studios being an exception. Many of the major studios such as Universal and Warner Bros. are located in nearby communities. But the magic of Hollywood itself remains, as though all the major motion picture studios of the world were clustered together in that small community on a shady lane grinding out film after film for the enjoyment of moviegoers everywhere.

Hollywood's existence, in part, is due to today's massive influx of tourists year after year. Tour buses seldom have an empty seat, and the sites such as Mann's (Grauman's) Chinese Theater with its world-famous forecourt where movie star hand- and footprints are preserved in cement is rarely without a visitor, even in the wee hours of any morning. Such is Hollywood. Such is an industry that promotes make-believe on a scale nearly incomprehensible.

Even the "stars" themselves have an interest in the locations where motion pictures were filmed. I had the pleasure to meet and talk with actress Betty Garrett recently. She enthusiastically revealed that she enjoyed visiting motion picture locations and that her husband, the late Larry Parks (*The Jolson Story* and *Jolson Sings Again,* etc.), was so fascinated with motion picture locations that he often took visiting relatives and friends to locations no matter what time of the day or night.

In this vein, as familiar as I am with the Los Angeles area and the hundreds upon hundreds of motion picture and television series production sites that are outside the studios, I still get a thrill simply in being where the greats of the industry plied their trade for the enjoyment of so many persons for so many decades.

The Downtown
Los Angeles Area

Beaches (1988)

Hospitals in the Los Angeles area profit not only from a steady flow of patients, but from Hollywood motion picture and television production companies as well. The reason film makers utilize some 50 area hospitals is simple. It is much more economical to film segments in such facilities than to construct extremely costly studio sets.

The average cost to motion picture and television producers for such on-location filming ranges from $3,000 to $5,000 per day. Lengthy filming for a feature motion picture can run as high as $150,000.

The massive California Medical Center near downtown Los Angeles was the site of this Bette Midler film as well as Meredith Baxter-Birney's *Lady Be Good* (1989) and television's *Favorite Son.*

Beaches is based on author Iris Rainer Dart's novel. Bette Midler and Barbara Hershey meet on a beach as children and keep a pen-pal relationship into adulthood. As adults they fall for the same man.

The California Medical Center is located at 1401 S. Grand Avenue, Los Angeles, east of the Harbor Freeway (110) and north of the Santa Monica Freeway (10).

Thomas Brothers Map reference: page 44 at B4. 1992 revised edition: page 634 at D6.

The Grand Avenue (west) side of the building seen in *Beaches* (1988) and *Lady Be Good* (1989). (Photo taken in 1989.)

The "old" entrance to the building seen in television's *Favorite Son*. (Photo taken in 1989.)

Choo-Choo! (1932)

Hanging around the railroad yards a little farther north of the round-house seen in the Our Gang comedy *Railroadin'* three years earlier in 1929, the Gang meets a group of orphans who sneaked away from a train stopped for a short time at the nearby railroad station. The Gang members and the orphans exchange clothing and the Gang takes the place of the orphans on the train for a hectic ride to a distant city. During the ride chaos erupts when animals escape from their cages in a freight car and a novelty salesman (Otto Fries) who's had a little too much to drink gives the Gang a suitcase full of fireworks.

The opening segment of this film was shot near the 1st Street Viaduct in downtown Los Angeles. The viaduct's distinctive stairway is evident in the film. The railroad station's rest area was the park-like setting where the Gang first met the orphans. The area was demolished along with the railroad station in the late 1930s.

This site was also seen in the 1930s in *Something to Sing About* (1937) and in the Laurel and Hardy comedy *Berth Marks* in 1929.

In *Something to Sing About,* Grand National Pictures cast "gangster" James Cagney in a spoof of the Hollywood film industry, taking full advantage of the actor's dancing ability. The plot of the film centered on a New York City bandleader Terry Rooney (Cagney) summoned to Hollywood to star in a musical. After the musical is completed, Rooney marries his girl (Evelyn Daw), then is forced to live as a bachelor on the orders of the head of the studio (Gene Lockhart) so female fans would not be disappointed in the rising star.

Cagney's train arrived at the same railroad station seen in the Our Gang film, near the 1st Street Viaduct.

Musical director C. Bakaleinikoff received an Academy Award nomination for best musical score in the film.

In *Berth Marks* (1929), Stan Laurel and Oliver Hardy are musicians who get a job in "Pottsville" and decide to go there by train. Then, in typical Laurel and Hardy fashion, the two almost miss the train, have great difficulty getting settled in their "single" berth, then debark in Pottsville minus their musical instrument. Please refer to the *Pigskin Palooka* section of this book for further information on the Pottsville location. The 1st Street Viaduct and the site of the old Santa Fe Railroad Station were also seen in a segment of television's *Wiseguy* in 1987.

The 1st Street Viaduct was completed in December of 1929, six months after *Berth Marks* was released on June 1, 1929. It was dedicated to the memory of Henry G. Parker. The mayor of Los Angeles at that time was George E. Cryer.

The Santa Fe Railroad Station is truly a part of Los Angeles/Hollywood history as the train carrying the body of screen legend Rudolph Valentino from New York arrived there in 1926. The hearse and the automobile caravan left the station's parking lot and slowly proceeded through Los Angeles streets to Hollywood Memorial Park Cemetery where Valentino was interred. The address of the cemetery is 6000 Santa Monica Boulevard. Note: Valentino, who died at age 31 of peritonitis from a ruptured appendix, rests in the cemetery's Hollywood Catholic Mausoleum, off of Corridor A, in Crypt 1205 near a beautiful stained glass window.

When the "new" Los Angeles Union Station opened in the late 1930s, the "old" Santa Fe Railroad Station was partially demolished and the site occupied by the Santa Fe Transportation Company, a trucking firm that was, in turn, replaced by a branch of the Southern California Rapid Transit District. The only hint of the grand old railroad station that now exists on the property is the main rail lines.

A view of this site can only be obtained by walking under the south side of the 1st Street Viaduct and looking east toward the Los Angeles River.

This film site is at 300 Santa Fe Avenue, south of the 1st Street Viaduct in downtown Los Angeles.

Thomas Brothers Map reference: page 44 at E3 (Santa Fe Railroad Station site). 1992 revised edition: page 634 at H4; page 34 at D4 (Cemetery); 1992 revised edition: page 593 at G6.

Top: The 1st Street Viaduct and the site of the "old" Santa Fe Railroad Station seen in *Choo-Choo!* (1932), *Berth Marks* (1929) and *Something to Sing About* (1937). (Photo taken in 1989.) *Bottom:* Beneath the 1st Street Viaduct where members of Our Gang frolicked in *Choo-Choo!* (Photo taken in 1984.)

The entrance to Hollywood Memorial Park Cemetery. (Photo taken in 1984.)

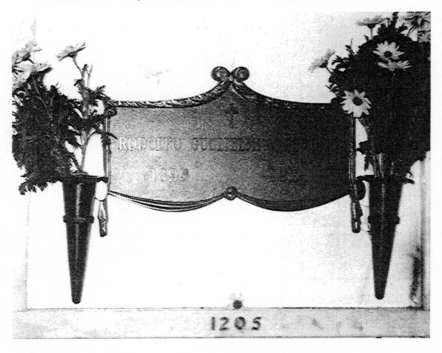

Crypt #1205, the final resting place of Rudolph Valentino. (Photo taken in 1990.)

Columbo (1989 to present)

Lt. Columbo (Peter Falk) is back, much to the delight of the many fans of the fictional detective who have been loyal followers over the decades.

Still clad in the sloppy raincoat first worn in the series' initial telecast of September 15, 1971, Columbo again chases the bad guys through the big city, assuring a fitting end to all concerned.

The "Sex and the Married Detective" episode aired on April 3, 1989, was shot in and around the beautiful Music Center Mall, a location familiar to millions of motion picture fans worldwide as the site of the bleachers that seat the most avid fans who wait days for the rare opportunity to view their favorite motion picture stars in person as they pass en route to the nearby Dorothy Chandler Pavilion, the site of many Academy Award ceremonies.

The Music Center Mall is located at 1st Street and Hope Street in downtown Los Angeles, south of the Hollywood Freeway (101) and east of the Harbor Freeway (110).

*Thomas Brothers Map reference: page 44 at D2. **1992 revised edition:** page 634 at F3.*

Both photos are of the north entrance to the pavilion, familiar to millions of persons as the entrance to many Academy Award ceremonies. This location was also seen in the "Sex and the Married Detective" episode of *Columbo*. (Photos taken in 1990.)

Copacabana (1985)

Singer/composer/songwriter Barry Manilow made his acting debut as a struggling songwriter who eventually hits it big in this rather campy salute to the Hollywood musicals of the 1940s.

Several nightclub scenes were filmed at the Variety Arts Center in downtown Los Angeles. This five-story building contains countless artifacts of the motion picture industry and is often used as a film location.

Dedicated in 1924, the building is architecturally historic as it was the first building constructed in Los Angeles with reinforced concrete as the mainstay. This is a primary reason it has withstood many major earthquakes and why it has not succumbed to the wrecker's ball.

The Variety Arts Center is solely dedicated to the acting profession. The film history contained within its walls is astounding and is arranged in a manner to allow the visitor to enjoy Hollywood's past no matter which level of the building is visited.

The main attractions are the Earl Carroll Lounge, the W.C. Fields Bar, the Masquers Theater, the Variety Arts Theater, the Music Library, the Theatrical Library, the Roof Garden Ballroom (seen in this film) and the Ed Wynn Bar & Lounge which was seen in a "back-in-time" episode of television's *Highway to Heaven* in 1987.

Other television series filmed here were *Cagney & Lacey*, *Falcon Crest* and *Murder, She Wrote*.

The Variety Arts Center Building (a.k.a. Friday Morning Club Building) is #196 in the city's Historical Cultural Monument listing.

The address is 940 S. Figueroa Street. This location is east of the Harbor Freeway (110) in downtown Los Angeles.

*Thomas Brothers Map reference: page 44 at C4. **1992 revised edition: page 634 at D5**.*

The Figueroa Street entrance to the Variety Arts Center. (Photo taken in 1987.)

Stage area of the center's Roof Garden seen in *Copacabana*. (Photo taken in 1989.)

The stairway of the center's Ed Wynn Comedy Cellar seen in a *Highway to Heaven* episode. (Photo taken in 1988.)

A stage prop in the Ed Wynn Comedy Cellar seen in a lengthy dance routine performed by Eleanor Powell in *Rosalie* (1937). (Photo taken in 1988.)

Days of Wine and Roses (1962)

The once proud hotel that served the citizens of Los Angeles and many of the city's visitors for decades, and the site of the closing segment of *Days of Wine and Roses,* is but a memory, replaced by a modern apartment complex that occupies the area west of Hill Street and east of Olive Street, from 2nd Street to 4th Street in downtown Los Angeles.

In this film drama, Jack Lemmon portrays a public relations man who tires of his work and turns to alcohol. Lee Remick plays his wife who also finds far too many moments of pleasure in the bottle. Both Lemmon and Remick were nominated for the Academy Award for their outstanding performances.

The hotel was transformed into a cheap bar for the scene. A smaller building immediately west of the structure was also seen in the film as Lemmon's cheap apartment.

In the closing scene of the film, Remick walks up the street, passes the bar, then enters the apartment building to pay a last visit to Lemmon and their daughter. She then leaves and retraces her route as Lemmon watches from a window.

The site of the hotel is above the 2nd Street Tunnel on the south side of the 2nd Street hill. (The 2nd Street hill is but one short block from Hill Street to Olive Street.) The hill is east of the Harbor Freeway (110) and south of 1st Street.

Please refer to the aerial photograph on page 15 (the upper photograph) that was taken prior to the construction of the apartment complex. The 2nd Street hill can be seen in the lower left section of the photograph.

The site of the old hotel seen in *Days of Wine and Roses* is immediately to the right of the hill where the cars are parked in a triangular-shaped parking area in the same photograph.

The lower photograph on page 15 shows the now extinct Clay Alley that ran behind the old hotel seen in the film from 2nd Street to 4th Street.

*Thomas Brothers Map reference: page 44 at D3. **1992 revised edition:** page 634 at F4.*

The site of the old hotel seen in *Days of Wine and Roses,* looking south from across 2nd Street, above the 2nd Street Tunnel.

Another view of the building that now occupies the site of the old hotel seen in the film.

Top: The site of the hotel seen in *Days of Wine and Roses* is the triangular parking area in the lower left section of this aerial photograph, behind the large office building. (Photo taken in 1977.) *Bottom:* A 1977 photograph of Clay Alley that ran behind the *Days of Wine and Roses* hotel from 2nd Street to 4th Street. This alley no longer exists.

Death Wish II (1981)

Segments of this film were shot in historic Olvera Street in downtown Los Angeles. Olvera Street is a part of Plaza Park which, in turn, was a part of the original Pueblo Land Grant. It was here that the city of Los Angeles was founded by eleven families on September 4, 1781, on the orders of then Governor Felipe de Neve. Plaza Park is #64 in the city's Historical Cultural Monument listing.

In this film (the sequel to the 1974 film *Death Wish*), Charles Bronson recreates his role of the New York City businessman who goes on a solo crusade to rid city streets of the baddies. He simply moves across the nation to Los Angeles to continue his vigilantism.

Segments of the comedy spoof *The Cool Ones* were also shot on Olvera Street in 1967 as well as scenes from 1981's *True Confessions*. In the latter, Robert De Niro and Robert Duvall star as two brothers. De Niro is a priest and Duvall a policeman. They are brought into conflict over the murder of a priest.

And the television industry did not forget this location as episodes of *CHiPs* and *Lou Grant* were also filmed here.

Olvera Street is north of the Los Angeles Civic Center, between Alameda Street and Main Street, at Sunset Boulevard, north of the Hollywood Freeway (101) and east of the Harbor Freeway (110).

*Thomas Brothers Map reference: page 44 at E2. **1992 revised edition:** page 634 at G3.*

Two views of Olvera Street seen in *Death Wish II* (1981), *The Cool Ones* (1967) and *True Confessions* (1981) as well as in television's *CHiPs* and *Lou Grant*. (Photos taken in 1989.)

Death Wish 4: The Crackdown (1987)

It seems as though Charles Bronson likes the Los Angeles thugs. In this fourth entry of the series he returns to the City of Angels, much grayer and a little meaner. His target is the drug trade and its elimination. The garage complex located at 7th Street and Wilshire Boulevard was seen in an exciting chase scene, as was most of the downtown area.

This site is located west of the Los Angeles Civic Center, on Bixel Street between 7th Street and Wilshire Boulevard, just west of the Harbor Freeway (110).

Thomas Brothers Map reference: page 44 at C3. 1992 revised edition: page 634 at D3.

The auto park structure located on the east side of Bixel Street, between 7th Street and Wilshire Boulevard seen in *Death Wish 4: The Crackdown.*

Dragnet (1969)

In this second feature film based on the popular television series, writer/producer/director/actor Jack Webb teamed with Harry Morgan to investigate a series of murders of models in Los Angeles.

Exterior filming for this motion picture was shot at the Police Administration Building (now renamed Parker Center in memory of the late Chief of Police William H. Parker) as were scenes from the original *Dragnet* motion picture in 1954 and many *Dragnet* television episodes. In fact, Webb began filming at this location shortly after the building was dedicated on September 12, 1955, and continued to do so until the *Dragnet* television series was cancelled on September 10, 1970.

It must be noted that Webb faithfully recreated many interior areas of Parker Center in his Mark VII, Ltd. production company studios for all interior filming. And the detail was astounding, looking exactly like Parker Center down to the oak furniture and police-oriented wall decorations.

Early *Dragnet* television episodes were filmed, in part, at the Los Angeles City Hall, the location of the Los Angeles Police Department's headquarters prior to 1970. Friday's police car exited and entered this building regularly, using the entrance located at the southeast corner facing Main Street, north of 1st Street. My father-in-law, George Mogelberg, was employed by the City of Los Angeles, holding the position of a guard at that time at that location, and was seen in many *Dragnet* television episodes and in the 1954 *Dragnet* motion picture. Please refer to *The Adventures of Superman* section of this book for the location.

Actor Dan Aykroyd starred in a comedy version of *Dragnet* in 1987. Many scenes for this motion picture were shot at Parker Center; the Los Angeles Street public entrance to the building and the San Pedro Street police entrance/exit were the primary locations.

Jack Webb also used the old Georgia Street Juvenile Division building for many exterior and interior scenes for his *Dragnet* television series, the obvious intent to maintain authentic locations to create an atmosphere as close to reality as possible for the viewing public.

This building, now demolished to make room for an expansion of the Los Angeles Convention Center complex, was originally the Georgia Street Receiving Hospital. It served the surrounding community before, during and after World War II until a more modern receiving hospital was opened on June 7, 1957. ·

The new facility, Central Receiving Hospital, was constructed at the cost of $1.5 million and was the brainchild of Dr. Charles Sebastian who lobbied civic leaders for over 20 years to attain his goal.

Jack Webb, without question, greatly contributed to making the Los Angeles Police Department world-famous through his excellent characterization of *Dragnet's* Sgt. Joe Friday both on radio and television in the 1940s, 1950s, 1960s and 1970s.

Webb's "tough cop" character was, in essence, carried on in television 14 years later in *Hunter,* a police drama that was also a takeoff on Clint Eastwood's "Dirty Harry" character that proved to be one of the biggest motion picture box-office draws of the 1970s and 1980s.

When *Hunter* was first telecast on September 18, 1984, the historic Culver City City Hall was the location of the police headquarters building where Rick Hunter (Fred Dryer) and his partner Dee Dee McCall (Stepfanie Kramer) were assigned. The two later relocated to the downtown Los Angeles area, in the massive police facility, Parker Center Police Headquarters. All exterior shots of Hunter's "new" home were taken there. Please refer to the *County Hospital* section of this book for further information on the Culver City City Hall.

Parker Center Police Headquarters is located at 150 North Los Angeles Street in downtown Los Angeles. The site of the Georgia Street Juvenile Division building is 1335 Georgia Street, south of Pico Boulevard, east of the Harbor Freeway (110) and north of the Santa Monica Freeway (10) near downtown Los Angeles.

Thomas Brothers Map reference: page 44 at D3 (Parker Center); 1992 revised edition: page 634 at G4; page 44 at B4 (Georgia Street Juvenile Building); 1992 revised edition: page 634 at D5.

The entrance to the Parker Center parking lot seen in *Dragnet* (1969) and in the *Dragnet* television series. (Photo taken in 1987.)

The main entrance to Parker Center seen in both *Dragnet* (1969) and *Dragnet* (1987) as well as in the *Dragnet* television series. (Photo taken in 1987.)

The San Pedro Street (back) entrance to Parker Center seen throughout the *Dragnet* television series and in *Dragnet* (1987). (Photo taken in 1987.)

The Georgia Street Juvenile Division building seen frequently in the *Dragnet* television series. (Photo taken in 1988 as demolition began.)

Fatal Vision (1984)

The City of Los Angeles long ago announced its determination to preserve its historic buildings. The Spring Street Towers, located at 650 S. Spring Street, are a classic example. Built in 1920, the 12-story structure is of the classic Beaux Arts style, complete with a rich façade of Indiana limestone and terra cotta. During its heyday, it was the Los Angeles headquarters of the Bank of America.

Scenes from *Fatal Vision* were shot in the building. The plot centers on the murder case in which ex–Green Beret captain Jeffery MacDonald was arrested and jailed for the murders of his wife and children.

Prizzi's Honor and *St. Elmo's Fire* were also filmed here in 1985. Jack Nicholson and Kathleen Turner starred in *Prizzi's Honor,* a black comedy about a Mafia hit-man who falls in love. In *St. Elmo's Fire,* Rob Lowe and Demi Moore star as college graduates who find that life away from school isn't exactly what they thought it would be, facing crisis after crisis.

Episodes from television's *Cagney & Lacey, Matlock, Hill Street Blues* and *Hardcastle & McCormick* were also shot here.

The Spring Street Towers are located at 650 S. Spring Street, Los Angeles, east of the Harbor Freeway (110) and south of the civic center.

*Thomas Brothers Map reference: page 44 at D3. **1992 revised edition:** page 634 at F5.*

The bank building located at 650 S. Spring Street in *Fatal Vision* (1984), *Prizzi's Honor* (1985), *St. Elmo's Fire* (1985) and the television series listed in this section. (Photos taken in 1989.)

Feet First (1930)

In this Harold Lloyd "talkie" film, the comic once again returns to the skyscrapers of downtown Los Angeles and scales a very high building. Oddly, this building, the Ninth and Broadway Building, located at 848 S. Broadway, is across the street from both buildings Lloyd utilized seven years earlier in *Safety Last:* the building on whose roof the famous façade was constructed for the "clock" scene (908 S. Broadway) and the Broadway Building (801 S. Broadway). Please refer to the *Safety Last* section of this book.

Although Lloyd appeared in all close-up scenes of this film, the person who risked his life on the building's exterior was stuntman Harvey Parry, an outstanding athlete who doubled for Lloyd in several films.

The Ninth and Broadway Building is located on the northeast corner of the intersection of 9th Street and Broadway in downtown Los Angeles and is east of the Harbor Freeway (110).

Thomas Brothers Map reference: page 44 at C4. 1992 revised edition: page 634 at E5.

The Ninth and Broadway Building, 848 S. Broadway, seen in *Feet First* (1930). (Photo taken in 1990.)

48 Hrs. (1982)

This hilarious film teams a convict (Eddie Murphy) with a detective (Nick Nolte) for two days in order to catch a pair of San Francisco cop killers. A prime scene occurs in a redneck bar where Murphy, to say the least, is a bit out of place. The duo somehow survive a hectic bar brawl and ramble on to complete their mission.

"Torchy's," the location used in this lengthy scene, is indeed a bar and the actual name is Torchy's. This bar was also seen with a rather mild crowd inside in the year 1999 in *Condor* (1986).

Torchy's is located at 218½ W. 5th Street in downtown Los Angeles.

Thomas Brothers Map reference: page 44 at D3. 1992 revised edition: page 634 at F4.

Torchy's Bar, a location of bar segments seen in *48 Hrs.* (1982) and *Condor* (1986). (Photo taken in 1989.)

Gangbusters (1952)

This short-lived television series was based on the popular radio program of the same name that was first broadcast in 1936 under the sponsorship of Palmolive Brushless Shaving Cream, one of the products offered to the American public in the 1930s. The radio program's producer/director/writer was Phillips H. Lord and the narrator was Colonel H. Norman Schwarzkopf, the father of General H. Norman Schwarzkopf of Desert Shield/Desert Storm fame.

The television program initially aired on March 20, 1952, and lasted only until December 25 of that year. The writer once again was Phillips H. Lord, who also did the narration.

The opening logo of the telecast depicted a platoon of uniformed police officers tramping to cadence which soon became the series' famous trademark.

This segment was filmed on the athletic field of the Los Angeles Police Academy during a graduation ceremony.

Segments of television's *Sledge Hammer!*, *The Oldest Rookie*, *Hill Street Blues* and *T.J. Hooker,* and the motion pictures *The New Centurions* (1972) and *The Rookies* (1972) were also filmed here.

Probably the most popular television series filmed at this location was *T.J. Hooker,* a police drama that was first telecast on March 13, 1982, and enjoyed a fairly good run to its last telecast on September 17, 1987.

William Shatner (*Star Trek's* Captain Kirk) portrayed T.J. Hooker, a uniformed police sergeant who gave up a detective position to return to the streets because he believed he was needed there more. His assignment was the Academy Precinct of the L.A.P.D.

The Academy Precinct's entrance, in reality, was the entrance to the pistol range at the Los Angeles Police Academy. The L.A.P.D. buildings were, in fact, on the lot of the television production company.

As a note of interest, one of my L.A.P.D. academy classmates was one Thomas J. Hooker, a husky man who enjoyed quite a career during his tenure as a policeman and, later, as a police sergeant. He told me quite frankly after the series first aired that he was convinced that not only was his name used in the development of the series, but some of his most famous adventures as well.

Within the L.A.P.D. Academy complex (immediately east of the pistol range entrance) are the famous Rock Gardens. The gardens were designed and built by the expert landscape artist François Scotti in 1937. They have a series of four pools and waterfalls as well as a small amphitheater for band and stage settings. The gardens are #110 in the city's Historical Cultural Monument listing.

Also on the academy grounds and unknown to most of the citizens of Los Angeles as well as to most of the citizens of the United States, for that matter, is a piece of Los Angeles city and Olympic Games history. It is a small building; one of the few remaining barracks buildings that housed athletes from around the world who competed in the 1932 Olympic Games held in the Los Angeles Memorial Coliseum. This building is now Classroom 7, located above the tiered parking area on the left (west) side of the entrance to the academy complex.

As a note of interest, the 1932 Olympic Village was located on the top of nearby Baldwin Hills, now a beautiful residential area.

The Los Angeles Police Academy is located at 1880 N. Academy Drive in Elysian Park, across the street from Dodger Stadium. There is an Academy Road exit on both the north and south lanes of the nearby Pasadena Freeway (110), just north of downtown Los Angeles. Academy Road leads to Academy Drive.

Thomas Brothers Map reference: page 35 at D5. 1992 revised edition: page 594 at G6.

The entrance to the Los Angeles Police Academy seen in *The Rookies* (1972) and in *The Oldest Rookie* (1987). (Photo taken in 1987.)

The stairway leading to the academy's classrooms seen in *The Rookies*. (Photo taken in 1987.)

The academy's athletic field seen in television's *Gangbusters* and in the motion picture *The New Centurions* (1972). (Photo taken in 1986.)

A 1932 Olympic Games barracks building, now Classroom #7. (Photo taken in 1986.)

The Spanish-style entrance to the Academy Precinct seen in television's *T.J. Hooker*. (Photo taken in 1989.)

Grease (1978)

I've been contacted by scores of John Travolta fans requesting that I list the location seen in the closing segments of *Grease* wherein a very dangerous and daring car race took place, headed by a defiant Travolta.

The entire scene was filmed in the cement bed of the Los Angeles River, the site of many motion picture and television series location shots.

The actual location where Travolta raced was between the 6th Street Viaduct and the 4th Street Viaduct, on the west side of the riverbed.

This location was also seen in a 1990 *Moonlighting* episode, a 1991 *Hunter* episode, in the 1990 motion picture *Curiosity Kills* and in *The Gumball Rally*, a wacky 1976 tale about adult speed demons participating in an annual auto race from New York to California. Oddly, the *Grease* car race was recreated at the same location virtually scene for scene in a *CHiPs* television episode in the early 1980s.

This film location can be viewed from either viaduct. Parking on viaducts, however, is not allowed. I suggest you park at the west side of either viaduct and walk the short distance to a location above the film site.

This location is west of the Santa Ana Freeway (5), between the Hollywood Freeway (101) and the Santa Monica Freeway (10).

*Thomas Brothers Map reference: page 44 at E4. **1992 revised edition:** page 634 at H5.*

Top: The west side of the Los Angeles River, looking north toward the 4th Street Viaduct, the location of the *Grease* car race. (Photo taken in 1986.) *Bottom:* The location under the 6th Street Viaduct where John Travolta agreed to take part in the race, and the location seen in the motion pictures and television series listed in this section. (Photo taken in 1986.)

L.A. Law (1986 to present)

When the show was first telecast on October 3, 1986, the offices of the firm were located at the Criminal Courts Building on Temple Street in downtown Los Angeles. After the initial season, the offices were moved to the Wells Fargo Building, a little farther south on Flower Street. Most of the cases involving individuals from the firm were held at the Los Angeles County Municipal Courts Building in downtown Los Angeles on Grand Avenue.

This critically acclaimed series was one of the few hits of the 1986 television season. Steve Bochco *(Hill Street Blues)* and former Deputy D.A. Terry Louise Fisher *(Cagney & Lacey)* were the creators.

The law firm of McKenzie Brackman Chaney Kuzak & Becker tackle all types of cases, representing the rich and the poor alike. The usual mix of office politics and sexual situations provide relief from the courtroom dramatics.

The Criminal Courts Building is located at 210 W. Temple Street and the Los Angeles County Municipal Courts Building at 110 N. Grand Avenue, both at *Thomas Brothers Map reference: page 44 at D2. 1992 revised edition: page 634 at G3.* The Wells Fargo Building is located at 444 S. Flower Street, *Thomas Brothers Map reference: page 44 at C3. 1992 revised edition: page 634 at E4.* Both locations are south of the Hollywood Freeway (101) and east of the Harbor Freeway (110).

The Criminal Courts Building is a *Matlock* favorite, serving as a court building in a 1989 episode and again as a court building in "The Celebrity," a 1991 *Matlock* thriller. The building was also seen in the 1990 television series *The Trials of Rosie O'Neill* as not only a court building but the Los Angeles City Hall.

As a note of interest, since I photographed the Wells Fargo Building, the property changed owners and the Wells Fargo stagecoach logo located near the top of the skyscraper was removed and replaced with the numbers 444, the Flower Street address of the building.

The Wells Fargo Building (center of photograph), the current location of the offices of *L.A. Law*. (Photo taken in 1989.)

The Los Angeles County Municipal Courts Building, the location seen in *L.A. Law*, *Matlock* and *The Trials of Rosie O'Neill*. (Photo taken in 1989.)

The entrance to the Criminal Courts Building seen in early episodes of *L.A. Law*. (Photo taken in 1989.)

A view of the building from the intersection of Temple Street and Spring Street. (Photo taken in 1989.)

Murder, She Wrote (1984 to present)

This very popular and highly rated detective drama was first telecast on September 30, 1984, with lovely Angela Lansbury in the role of Jessica Fletcher, a former school teacher who attained success in later life as an author of mystery novels.

Whether in her mythical town of Cabot Cove in New England, or in any other city or community in the United States she visits, murder somehow follows.

Cabot Cove, in reality, is on the Universal Studios back lot and the rest of the United States is either at the studio complex or on the streets of Los Angeles.

One such location seen occasionally in this series is the old Highland Park Police Station as a police station. This facility served the Highland Park area of Los Angeles through two world wars and a lot of community change. Abandoned due to a modern police facility activated nearby, the building was bought by a motion picture production company which regularly leases it to other production companies who are after "authentic" exterior and interior shots of a police facility.

This location was also seen in television's *MacGyver* and in segments of Carol Burnett's television movie *Fresno* (1986).

Another favorite location for *Murder, She Wrote* producers is the Biltmore Hotel in downtown Los Angeles. It has often been said that the Biltmore Hotel *is* Los Angeles as it so dominates the heart of the city.

This magnificent structure was opened on October 1, 1923, and constructed on land once a part of the original four square leagues owned by the Pueblo of Los Angeles. The interior of the building has many beautiful works of art that attract the attention of not only visitors and guests, but motion picture and television production companies as well. It is #60 in the city's Historical Cultural Monument listing.

Segments of the motion pictures *Beverly Hills Cop* (1984), *Ghostbusters* (1984) and *Kinjite* (1989) were filmed at the hotel.

In *Beverly Hills Cop*, Eddie Murphy portrayed a Detroit police officer in search of a killer. In *Ghostbusters*, "Saturday Night Live" alumni Dan Aykroyd and Bill Murray zipped around "New York City" in search of demons. In *Kinjite* (Japanese translation: "Forbidden Subjects"), Charles Bronson portrayed a Los Angeles Police detective investigating the kidnapping of the daughter of a Los Angeles-based Japanese businessman.

Early Hollywood motion pictures were also filmed here. The hotel appeared in the opening segment of Bert Wheeler and Robert Woolsey's 1931 comedy *Cracked Nuts* as an apartment building that housed Edna May Oliver and Wheeler's girl, the lovely Dorothy Lee.

Other television series segments filmed here were for *A Year in the Life, Falcon Crest, Highway to Heaven, J.J. Starbuck* and for the "Blues in the Night" episode of *Jake and the Fatman* that aired in 1988. Scenes for a 1989 *Perry Mason* television movie were also shot here.

The Olive Street entrance to the Biltmore Hotel was the location where the infamous *Black Dahlia* (Elizabeth Short) was last seen as she exited the building, walked north on the busy sidewalk and into Los Angeles crime history. Her mutilated body was found days later on the morning of January 15, 1947, in a field near Norton Avenue and 39th Street in the Leimert section of the city, many miles south of the Biltmore Hotel. The crime remains unsolved.

The old Highland Park Police Station is located at 6045 York Boulevard, near Figueroa Street, west of the Pasadena Freeway (110). It is #274 in the city's Historical Cultural Monument listing.

The Biltmore Hotel is located at 506 S. Grand Avenue, east of the Harbor Freeway (110). Note: If the (110) for both the Pasadena Freeway and the Harbor Freeway seems a bit confusing, the Pasadena Freeway is the northern extension of the Harbor Freeway.

As a note of interest, the location where Elizabeth Short's body was discovered succumbed to progress. A contractor constructed a housing development on the site in the early 1960s.

Thomas Brothers Map reference: page 36 at C1 (Old Highland Park Police Station); 1992 revised edition: page 595 at D1; page 44 at C3 (Biltmore Hotel); 1992 revised edition: page 634 at E4; page 51 at C1 (Black Dahlia crime site); 1992 revised edition: page 673 at E2.

Both photos are of the "old" Highland Park Police Station seen in television's *Murder, She Wrote* and *MacGyver* and in the motion picture *Fresno* (1986). (Photos taken in 1986.)

Top: The Olive Street entrance to the Biltmore Hotel seen in *Murder, She Wrote* and in the motion pictures and television series listed in this section. (Photo taken in 1990.)
Bottom: Looking north on Norton Avenue toward Coliseum Street. Elizabeth Short's body was found on the west (left) side of Norton Avenue in weeds near the sidewalk. (Photo taken in 1990.)

Never Give a Sucker an Even Break (1941)

This motion picture is one of the few films ever made that was absolutely hilarious with virtually no plot.

Simply, W.C. Fields (as himself) relates a story to a motion picture producer (Franklin Pangborn) revolving around a central character (Fields) who falls out of an airplane, lands in a small country called Ruritania, meets a girl who has never seen a man and on and on it goes.

Oddly, this comedy over the decades has been elevated to a cult status by film buffs simply because it proved to be Fields' last starring role as well as one of his best performances before the camera.

Near the film's conclusion, Fields drives his niece (Gloria Jean) to a department store. He decides to wait in his car while she shops. Suddenly, a heavy but not pregnant woman rushes from the department store and asks Fields to take her to a nearby maternity hospital. Thinking the woman is about to deliver and unaware that she is only late for a visit, Fields volunteers.

The hectic drive to the hospital was filmed in East Los Angeles on and near the 7th Street Viaduct. Fields' car roared onto the viaduct at its east end and exited at its west end, skidding to a stop at the intersection of 7th Street and Santa Fe Avenue to get directions from a traffic officer.

The street scenes filmed immediately thereafter were on Mission Road and on Santa Fe Avenue, north of the 7th Street Viaduct, between the viaduct and the 1st Street Viaduct. The west terminus of the 7th Street Viaduct is evident in the film, its distinctive decorative columns and railing prominent. Today, however, the railing has been remodeled and the spaces between the railing posts filled with cement.

As this lengthy scene continues, Fields wildly drives across a second bridge, his car now coupled to the extended ladder of a fire engine racing to an emergency call. This film site is several miles west of the 7th Street Viaduct in the Atwater section of Los Angeles near the city of Glendale. This bridge is the Glendale-Hyperion Viaduct. The scene concludes with a spectacular traffic accident near the entrance to the maternity hospital.

The 7th Street Viaduct spans the Los Angeles River near downtown Los Angeles. It is bounded by Myers Street on the east and Santa Fe Avenue on the west.

The Glendale-Hyperion Viaduct also spans the Los Angeles River as well as the Golden State Freeway (5). It is bounded by Greensward Road on the north and Ettrick Street on the south. It is #164 in the city of Los Angeles' Historical Cultural Monument listing.

Thomas Brothers Map reference: page 44 at E5 and F5 (7th Street Viaduct). 1992 revised edition: page 634 at H6; page 35 at B2 (Glendale-Hyperion Viaduct); 1992 revised edition: page 594 at D2.

The west end of the 7th Street Viaduct where W.C. Fields' car roared toward a hospital in *Never Give a Sucker an Even Break.* (Photo taken in 1990.)

The intersection of 7th Street and Santa Fe Avenue where W.C. Fields' car skidded to a stop. (Photo taken in 1990.)

The Glendale-Hyperion Viaduct, the second bridge W.C. Fields crossed en route to a hospital. (Photo taken in 1990.)

Pennies from Heaven (1981)

An unusual mix of comedy, drama and even murder set in the gloomy years of the Great Depression with lavish musical numbers reminiscent of the spectacular Hollywood productions of that era comprise the bulk of this lengthy Steve Martin "epic."

Many of the location scenes were filmed at, near or under the 4th Street Viaduct, east of downtown Los Angeles.

The viaduct underpass where both Steve Martin and Vernel Bagneris met the blind girl is on the east side of Santa Fe Avenue. The "love scene" between Martin and co-star Bernadette Peters that took place in Martin's car was filmed under the viaduct on the west side of Santa Fe Avenue. This is also the location where where the motorcycle policemen arrested Martin for the murder of the blind girl.

Santa Fe Avenue became a San Francisco street a few years later in a police pursuit in *Badge of the Assassin* (1985), the 4th Street Viaduct clearly visible in the distance.

The location for both films is on Santa Fe Avenue between 4th Street and 6th Street, east of Alameda Street and west of the Los Angeles River.

Thomas Brothers Map reference: page 44 at E4. 1992 revised edition: page 634 at H5.

Top: The west side of Santa Fe Avenue, under the 4th Street Viaduct, where the Steve Martin and Bernadette Peters love scene was shot in *Pennies from Heaven* (1981). (Photo taken in 1986.) *Bottom:* The east side of Santa Fe Avenue at the 4th Street Viaduct where the blind girl was murdered in *Pennies from Heaven* (1981). (Photo taken in 1986.)

Santa Fe Avenue approaching the 4th Street Viaduct seen in *Pennies from Heaven* (1981) and in *Badge of the Assassin* (1985). (Photo taken in 1988.)

Perfect Strangers (1986 to 1992)

An immigrant from the Mediterranean island of Mypos (Bronson Pinchot) comes to the shores of the United States and heads directly to Chicago and an unexpected and unannounced meeting with his American cousin (Mark Linn-Baker) during the first telecast of this comedy series on March 25, 1986. The two somehow adjust to each other and television comedy history is made.

During the initial year of this series, both Balki (Pinchot) and "Cousin Larry" (Linn-Baker) lived and worked in the same apartment building. Their place of employment was on the first floor, the Ritz Discount Department Store, a used furniture store owned by Ernie Sabella that had a "going out of business sale" each month. Their modest apartment was located directly above the department store.

This "Chicago" building is actually the Santa Rita Hotel, a 4-story brick building located on the southern fringe of downtown Los Angeles, east of the Harbor Freeway (110) and north of the Santa Monica Freeway (10). The address is 1100 S. Main Street.

In this television series the hotel's name is the "Caldwell Hotel." Larry and Balki's apartment is located on the third floor just to the right of the fire escape overlooking Main Street.

Later, however, the two cousins moved to a new address, an apartment building that looks similar to the one on Main Street. I contacted the production company. A spokesperson informed me that the two moved "next door" to a different apartment but that the exterior shots of the apartment building are now of an apartment building in Chicago.

Thomas Brothers Map reference: page 44 at C4. 1992 revised edition: page 634 at E5.

The Santa Rita Hotel, the home of Larry and Balki in television's *Perfect Strangers*. (Photo taken in 1987.)

The Main Street side of the hotel. Larry and Balki's apartment is on the 3rd floor to the right of the fire escape. (Photo taken in 1987.)

Prince of Darkness (1987)

A college instructor (Victor Wong), responding to a plea from a priest (Donald Pleasence), asks students from his class to accompany him to the church to investigate the possibility of the Devil occupying the cellar of the church. The Devil, in fact, does occupy the cellar, sealed in a glass container that is estimated to be over 7 million years old. Somehow the Devil squirts a student with a green liquid and the fun begins, complete with zombies swarming about the exterior of the church. The film ends as the hero (Jameson Parker) awakens from a deep sleep.

The site selected for this film was an actual church building in downtown Los Angeles, located at 120 N. San Pedro Street. Although the building is now abandoned, it served the area proudly for decades, housing the Protestant Congregation for the Japanese-American citizens of Los Angeles. Dedicated in 1923 as the Japanese Union Church of Los Angeles, it now bears the name of St. Godard's Church, so inscribed on a fading sign near the entrance.

. The Japanese Union Church of Los Angeles is #312 in the city's Historical Cultural Monument listing.

This site is south of the Hollywood Freeway (101).

Thomas Brothers Map reference: page 44 at D3. 1992 revised edition: page 634 at G4.

Both photographs are of the St. Godard's Church, a primary location of *Prince of Darkness*. Note the downtown Los Angeles skyscrapers in the distance in the bottom photograph. (Photos taken in 1990.)

The walkway on the south side of St. Godard's Church where zombies lingered in *Prince of Darkness*. (Photo taken in 1990.)

Pups Is Pups (1930)

The members of Our Gang, without funds for an entry fee, plot to enter their pets in a pet show with the hope to win the "Big Prize." Their "ticket" into the huge auditorium is Gang member "Farina" (Allen Hoskins) who happens to work in the display room as a page.

As the Gang preen their assortment of pets, "Wheezer" (Bobby Hutchins) can't find his puppies as they have the annoying habit of responding to the sound of a bell. And there are many bells in the neighborhood, — the ice cream man, an ambulance, passing trains, etc.

The first half of this Hal Roach Studios comedy is dedicated to Wheezer's search for the puppies.

The streets and sidewalks of the east side of downtown Los Angeles were the primary film sites. Today, over six decades later, a stately brick wall seen in the film still stands. It parallels a sidewalk on Center Street, between Ducommun Street and Commercial Street, once a barrier protecting the gas works seen in the film.

A building seen in the film immediately after Wheezer tosses a rock through an apartment building window still stands. It is now an auto repair shop located on the northwest corner of Temple Street and Center Street, a few yards south of the brick wall. The address is 749 E. Temple Street.

This excellent comedy concludes as Wheezer is finally reunited with his puppies on the steps of a church, thanks to the sudden ringing of the church bells.

The church seen in this film is St. Brendan's. It is located many miles west of downtown Los Angeles at the intersection of 3rd Street and Van Ness Avenue in Los Angeles, west of the Hollywood Freeway (101). The film site (the entrance to the church) faces Van Ness Avenue, just south of 3rd Street.

St. Brendan's church was also the setting two years later (1932) for yet another Our Gang comedy. It was seen in the closing segment of *Birthday Blues* as "Spanky" (George McFarland), Dickie Moore (Spanky's brother in the film) and the parents (Hooper Atchley and Lillian Rich) approach the entrance on the sidewalk on the east side of Van Ness Avenue, immediately south of the church.

As a note of interest, the final scenes of *The War of the Worlds* (1953) were filmed at this church even though the exterior of the First United Methodist Church of Hollywood at 6817 Franklin Avenue in Hollywood was used for distant shots.

Many other *War of the Worlds* locations are listed in this book. Please refer to the appropriate section.

*Thomas Brothers Map reference: page 44 at E3 (brick wall and building); **1992 revised edition:** page 634 at H4; page 43 at D1 (church); **1992 revised edition:** page 633 at G1.*

The downtown Los Angeles Temple Street building seen in *Pups Is Pups*. (Photo taken in 1986.)

The brick wall and sidewalk at the intersection of Center Street and Commercial Street seen in *Pups Is Pups*. (Photo taken in 1986.)

Top: The Van Ness Avenue entrance to the church seen in *Pups Is Pups* (1930), *Birthday Blues* (1932) and in the closing scenes of *The War of the Worlds* (1953). (Photo taken in 1990.) *Bottom:* The steeple of the church seen in *Pups Is Pups* (1930) and *Birthday Blues* (1932). (Photo taken in 1988.)

The Van Ness Avenue neighborhood, south of the church, seen in *Birthday Blues*. (Photo taken in 1987.)

Quincy, M.E. (1976 to 1983)

Located in the Little Tokyo section of Los Angeles, this very beautiful Higashi Hongwanji Buddhist Temple was dedicated on November 7, 1976. The church, however, was founded in 1904 and has moved several times before finally resettling in Little Tokyo. The temple retains as much of the architectural design of Japan as possible, including 40,000 "Kawara" roof tiles imported from Japan, which is extremely attractive to the motion picture and television industries.

Segments of this television series were filmed here. First telecast on October 3, 1976, *Quincy, M.E.* lasted until September 5, 1983. It was a police drama starring Jack Klugman as a physician who gave up his practice to join the Los Angeles County Coroner's Office as a medical examiner (M.E.). During his tenure at the office, he discovered that many "normal" deaths were, in fact, murders which cast the man more as a detective than a pathologist. His adventures led him into virtually every sector of the city, including Little Tokyo and this temple.

The church's former location, the Higashi Hongwanji Temple at 1st Street and Central Avenue in Little Tokyo, was dedicated in 1925 and was one of the original religious buildings serving Oriental Americans in the Los

Angeles area. The temple is #313 in the city's Historical Cultural Monument listing.

The "new" temple seen in the television segment is located at 505 E. 3rd Street. The "old" temple is located a few blocks north on the northwest corner of 1st Street and Central Avenue. It is now a museum.

Both locations are south of the Hollywood Freeway (101).

Thomas Brothers Map reference: page 44 at E3 (both temples); **1992 revised edition: page 634 at G4.**

The original Hongwanji Buddhist Temple. Constructed in 1924, it is now a museum and #313 in the city's Historical Cultural Monument listing. (Photo taken in 1989.)

Both photographs are of the "new" Hongwanji Buddhist Temple seen in television's *Quincy, M.E.* (Photos taken in 1989.)

Railroadin' (1929)

Our Gang's Joe Cobb and "Chubby" (Norman Chaney) take the Gang to the railroad yards to visit their dad (Otto Fries) who is an engineer. "Farina" (Allen Hoskins), of course, tags along. While at the railroad yards, Farina falls asleep and the plot of this film then revolves around his dream sequence that places the Gang in a runaway train.

The opening segment of this film was shot at a roundhouse located in the Santa Fe railroad yards near downtown Los Angeles. The "runaway train" scenes were shot on the railroad tracks that parallel the nearby Los Angeles River, north of the roundhouse. An arched bridge is seen several times in the film as the runaway train passes under it. It is the Olympic Boulevard Bridge.

The roundhouse still stands today, virtually unchanged. It is located north of Washington Boulevard and east of Santa Fe Avenue in the Santa Fe railroad yards.

As an item of interest, the Los Angeles River is the primary reason the Pueblo of Los Angeles was founded near Sunset Boulevard and Alameda Street. Once a source of nourishment for Indians, the river now is generally dry, serving a purpose when the winter rains come to the area. Historically, it is the only river in the United States whose course was established by a city ordinance.

Additionally, the Olympic Boulevard Bridge was dedicated in 1925 in the memory of Caspar De Portola, the first governor of the state of California.

These locations are south of the Santa Monica Freeway (10).

*Thomas Brothers Map reference: page 44 at F6. **1992 revised edition: page 674 at J1.***

Both photographs are of the roundhouse in the Santa Fe Railroad yards seen in the opening segment of *Railroadin'*. (Photos taken in 1984.)

The Olympic Boulevard Bridge, south of the roundhouse, seen in the "runaway train" segment of *Railroadin'*. (Photo taken in 1984.)

The 6th Street Viaduct, south of the Olympic Boulevard Bridge, also seen in the "runaway train" segment of *Railroadin'*. (Photo taken in 1984.)

The Ray Bradbury Theater (1990 to present)

This television series, hosted by the prolific writer Ray Bradbury, proved to be one of the few successes of the 1990 television season.

Each half-hour segment opens with a view of a wrought iron encased elevator rising briefly, then stopping. A shadow of a man then eases from the elevator and footsteps are heard approaching an office door. The man enters the office and a husky male voice begins: "People ask: 'Where do you get your ideas?' Right here. All of this is mine. I'll never starve here. I'm Ray Bradbury." Bradbury now enters a cluttered section of the office and begins his eerie tale.

The elevator and the office are situated in a downtown Los Angeles landmark, the Bradbury Building, a building chosen by Bradbury for the opening scenes of the television series for the obvious reason.

A person visiting this film location should be prepared to step back in time. Completed in 1893, this building is a tribute to the city's Victorian past. Five stories high, its ceiling is capped by a 50-by-120 foot skylight. The interior of the structure is a combination of brick, tile and metal. Two open cage elevators scurry up and down exposed elevator shafts, taking Bradbury and others to iron-grilled balconies that provide access to Bradbury's office and other offices scattered throughout the building.

Segments of the 1990 television movie *The Dreamer of Oz* were also filmed here. This motion picture was based on the life of L. Frank Baum, the man who authored the imaginative story "The Wonderful Wizard of Oz," that inspired the classic 1939 film *The Wizard of Oz*. In this television movie, the Bradbury Building housed the Chicago, Illinois, office of George Hill Publishers, the publishing company who first published Baum's work.

Many segments of the 1982 film *Blade Runner* were filmed here. The building is prominent throughout the film, most memorably as the locale of the dynamic conclusion of the film wherein Harrison Ford kills Daryl Hannah, and Rutger Hauer fights Ford only to save Ford's life shortly before his life ends.

As a "Victorian" building, this location was a "must" for several scenes in the motion picture classic *The White Cliffs of Dover*, a 1944 wartime film that starred the late Irene Dunne who gave an outstanding performance as an American woman living in England who loses her husband during World War I and her son in World War II. George Fosley received an Academy Award nomination for cinematography in the film.

The Bradbury Building is #6 in the city's Historical Cultural Monument listing. It is located on the southeast corner of 3rd Street and Broadway in downtown Los Angeles, east of the Harbor Freeway (110).

*Thomas Brothers Map reference: page 44 at D3. **1992 revised edition:** page 634 at F4.*

The Broadway entrance to the Bradbury Building. (Photo taken in 1986.)

The building's 1st floor lobby seen in *The White Cliffs of Dover*. (Photo taken in 1986.)

The building's ornate iron balconies seen in *White Cliffs of Dover* (1944) and *Blade Runner* (1982). (Photo taken in 1986.)

The building's open cage elevator seen in television's *The Ray Bradbury Theater* and in *The Dreamer of Oz* (1990). (Photo taken in 1986.)

Rocky (1976)

This Cinderella story of a Philadelphia boxer (Sylvester Stallone) who gets a shot at the heavyweight championship of the world won an Academy Award for Best Picture.

Even though many Philadelphia locations were used during filming, some were in Los Angeles, a primary one being the Olympic Auditorium near downtown Los Angeles.

The building's original seating capacity of 15,300 when dedicated on August 5, 1925, made it the largest auditorium ever built specifically for boxing in the western United States.

As expected, the scheduled events at the auditorium attracted a steady flow of Los Angeles citizens which included many from the entertainment industry from Al Jolson to Sylvester Stallone who would eventually star in this film and the successful sequels that followed.

Many of Stallone's boxing scenes in this film were shot here as were scenes for *Requiem for a Heavyweight* (1962).

Rocky earned an Academy Award for John G. Avilsen in the category of Best Director. Many Academy Award nominations were also received, i.e. Stallone for Best Actor; Talia Shire for Best Actress; Burgess Meredith for Best Supporting Actor; Stallone again for Best Screenplay written directly for the screen.

The Olympic Auditorium is located at 1801 S. Grand Avenue, south of the Santa Monica Freeway (10) and east of the Harbor Freeway (110).

*Thomas Brothers Map reference: page 44 at B5. **1992 revised edition:** page 634 at D6.*

A view of the Olympic Auditorium on Grand Avenue looking north toward 18th Street. (Photo taken in 1988.)

The Olympic Auditorium's Grand Avenue entrance. (Photo taken in 1987.)

Safety Last (1923)

According to the majority of motion picture historians, Harold Lloyd was the "third genius of the silent screen trilogy." This deserved compliment ranks him just behind film immortals Charlie Chaplin and Buster Keaton.

Of the more than 200 films Lloyd made, this film is remembered as by far his best. The still photograph of him hanging from the hands of a very large clock affixed to the side of a skyscraper is one of the most famous photographs in motion picture history.

For decades this comedic genius was credited with doing the daring stunt himself, hanging from the clock hands on the side of an actual skyscraper with nothing but thin air between him and the street many stories below. A great bit of Hollywood hype, but a myth.

The lengthy scene was filmed in downtown Los Angeles. Many of the structures seen in the film exist today, some seven decades later. Even the "skyscraper" where the famous clock scene was filmed still exists. It was one of three buildings Lloyd used as one building to film his single climb from the sidewalk to the roof. This was necessary for proper camera angles to give the illusion of a great increase in height.

Lloyd created another illusion. Even though the buildings he used appear to be on the same side of the street as adjoining buildings, they were not. Clever camera angles created the illusion of all buildings in individual scenes being next to each other.

The first building Lloyd used was located on the south of Olympic Boulevard, in the "Y" area between Broadway and Broadway Place. This building was demolished many years ago and a parking lot now occupies the space. Lloyd had a façade (movie set) of a building, complete with a large clock, constructed on the roof. The distance from the roof to the top of the façade was but a few feet. Thick mattresses were placed on the roof directly under the façade to soften a fall, just in case. Lloyd, however, did not fall during filming.

As the scene progressed and Lloyd climbed higher, the façade was moved to a taller building one block north on Broadway. This building's address is 908 S. Broadway. It still stands but is now abandoned. The street "far below" in the scene is Broadway, between 8th Street and 9th Street. The multi-story building that appears to be next to Lloyd's façade is the Broadway Building. It too still stands today. Its address is 801 S. Broadway. As a note of interest, the opposite (west) side of this building (830 S. Hill Street) was seen in the horror classic *War of the Worlds*. Please refer to the *War of the Worlds* section of this book.

The façade was again moved to the roof of a taller building three blocks north for the final scene. This building still stands today on the southeast corner of the intersection of 6th Street and Broadway. Its address is 610 S.

Broadway. The camera angle was east down 6th Street toward Spring Street. One building seen in several shots is virtually unchanged today. It is located on the northeast corner of 6th Street and Spring Street. Its address is 560 S. Spring Street.

Harold Lloyd's comedic genius over the decades that spanned the silent films to the "talkies" garnered him but one Oscar. He received the "honorary" award in 1952 for being a master comedian as well as a good citizen.

All locations are east of the Harbor Freeway (110).

Thomas Brothers Map reference: page 44 at C4 (801 and 908 S. Broadway & Olympic Blvd. and Broadway); 1992 revised edition: page 634 at E5; page 44 at D3 (6th and Broadway & 6th and Spring Street); *1992 revised edition: page 634 at F4.*

Top: The site of the *first* building used in Harold Lloyd's hanging from the clock scene in *Safety Last*. It is now a parking lot (the triangle in the center of the photograph). The façade (prop) of a building was constructed on the building's roof. (Photo taken in 1982.) *Bottom:* The intersection of Broadway and Olympic Boulevard seen in Lloyd's attempt to get to the roof of the *first* building in *Safety Last*. (Photo taken in 1990.)

Top: The *second* building used by Lloyd in the hanging from the clock scene in *Safety Last.* The prop façade and the prop clock were located on the building's roof, facing the rear of the building. (Photo taken in 1990.) *Bottom:* Broadway, between 8th Street and 9th Street, as seen from the *second* building in *Safety Last.* (Photo taken in 1990.)

Top: The *third* building and the roof area of the building used by Lloyd for the final hanging from the clock scene in *Safety Last.* (Photo taken in 1990.) *Bottom:* The *final* scene of *Safety Last,* looking east on 6th Street toward the building on the northeast corner of 6th Street and Spring Street (560 S. Spring Street). (Photo taken in 1990.)

Sledge Hammer! (1986 to 1988)

Detective Inspector Sledge Hammer (David Rasche) and his partner, Officer Dori Doreau (Anne-Marie Martin) began their search for criminals in the series' first telecast on September 23, 1986. The fearless duo hung up their handcuffs after the last telecast on June 30, 1988. In between they virtually wrecked the city of Los Angeles and ruined the police department.

This tongue-in-cheek police comedy was primarily filmed in the Los Angeles area. Many buildings were used regularly, the most familiar one to viewers being Sledge's apartment where he seldom went during the day but nearly always slept at night, cuddled next to his chrome plated, pearl handled .357 Magnum. The building that appeared as Sledge's apartment is located at 681 S. Burlington Avenue, north of 7th Street and west of the Harbor Freeway (110) near downtown Los Angeles. It is an apartment building.

The police station Sledge and Dori was assigned to is one block north and nine blocks east of Sledge's apartment building and is not a police station. It is an office building and surprisingly intact considering Sledge's antics throughout the series.

The police station (office building) is located at 1125 W. 6th Street, west of the Harbor Freeway (110) near downtown Los Angeles.

Thomas Brothers Map reference: page 44 at B2 (apartment building); 1992 revised edition: page 634 at C3; page 44 at C2 (police station); 1992 revised edition: page 634 at D3.

Sledge Hammer's apartment building seen throughout the *Sledge Hammer!* television series. (Photo taken in 1990.)

Sledge Hammer's police station seen throughout the television series. (Photo taken in 1990.)

Them! (1954)

Radiation emitted from atomic explosions in the southwestern part of the United States caused mutations in ants that made them grow into giants. These monsters soon swarmed into Los Angeles and the city's enormous storm drain system.

A very young James Arness teamed with James Whitmore and Edmund Gwenn to pinpoint the swarm's exact underground location so they could be destroyed before they reproduced and caused havoc within the city and throughout the surrounding communities.

The tunnel the ants used to enter the storm drain system exists today, virtually unchanged since this motion picture was filmed there. It is actually an access tunnel to the Los Angeles River from nearby Santa Fe Avenue, running directly under the 6th Street Viaduct.

The tunnel has also become popular with television movie and series production companies. It was seen in segments of the television movies *The Annihilator* (1986) and *Condor* (1986) and in the television series *Moonlighting* (1986) and *The Oldest Rookie* (1987).

The film location is under the 6th Street Viaduct, east of Santa Fe Avenue at the Los Angeles River channel in Los Angeles.

*Thomas Brothers Map reference: page 44 at E4. **1992 revised edition:** page 634 at H5.*

Top: The Los Angeles River (east) entrance to the tunnel seen in *Them!* (1954), *The Annihilator* (1986) and *Condor* (1986) and in television's *Moonlighting* and *The Oldest Rookie*. (Photo taken in 1986.) *Bottom:* The Santa Fe Avenue (west) entrance to the tunnel seen in *Moonlighting* and *The Oldest Rookie*. (Photo taken in 1986.)

Three's Company (1977 to 1984)

This popular situation comedy television series was first telecast on March 15, 1977, and concluded its lengthy run on September 18, 1984.

A simple plot of two young single women in search of a roommate turns confusing and extremely funny when they find the "new" roommate asleep in their bathtub the morning after a going-away party the two (Joyce DeWitt and Suzanne Somers) tossed for their last roommate. The new roommate is John Ritter.

The opening titles seen in the early years of this series were filmed at the Los Angeles Zoo, a popular location for motion picture and television production companies. But don't look for the familiar "Los Angeles Zoo" sign seen in the early titles, however, as it was demolished during remodeling in the early 1980s.

During the latter years of the series' run, the opening and closing titles were filmed at the Santa Monica Pier. Please refer to the *Inside Daisy Clover* section of this book for further information.

John Ritter continued in the *Three's Company* role of Jack Tripper with a new roommate (Mary Cadorette) in the situation comedy sequel *Three's a Crowd* that ran from September 25, 1984, to September 19, 1985.

Segments of television's *The Incredible Hulk*, *CHiPs*, *The Beverly Hillbillies* and the motion picture *Body and Soul* (1981) were also filmed at this location.

The zoo is located at 5333 Zoo Drive in Griffith Park, south of the Ventura Freeway (134) and west of the Golden State Freeway (5) in Los Angeles.

*Thomas Brothers Map reference: page 25 at A3. **1992 revised edition:** page 564 at B4.*

Both photographs are of the entrance to the Los Angeles Zoo seen in the opening credits of television's *Three's Company*. (Photos taken in 1987.)

The War of the Worlds (1953)

This sci-fi drama relating to a Martian invasion of our planet was adapted from H.G. Wells' classic story. In this film entry, the city of Los Angeles was a primary target. The Martians, not at all friendly, immediately begin destroying the city with deadly ray guns. The spectacular special effects created for this film won an Academy Award Oscar for Best Special Effects for the legendary science-fiction director/producer George Pal.

Many Los Angeles locations were used. The massive United States Government District Court Building located at 312 N. Spring Street became the "Armed Forces Public Information Office." It was here that the armed forces "brass" mapped strategy to destroy the Martians and save the Earth.

The caravan of military vehicles carrying the brass to this building approached, traveling east on Aliso Street, then turning south on Main Street. The Main Street entrance to the building was seen in the film.

In a later scene, actor Gene Barry (the star of the film) wandered through a deserted street in the heart of the city. This location is the intersection of 8th Street and Hill Street. The building most prominent, an office building, is located on the northeast corner. The address is 760 S. Hill Street. A bit farther south of this building, at 830 S. Hill Street is the Broadway Building, also prominent in the same scene. Please refer to the *Safety Last* section of this book for additional information on this film location.

The final scenes of this Martian attack of terror were filmed at St. Brendan's Church at 3rd Street and Van Ness Avenue. Please refer to the *Pups Is Pups* section of this book for additional information on this film location.

The United States Government District Court Building was also seen in *Oh, God! Book II* (1980) as a court building where a judge (Wilfred Hyde-White) ruled on whether God's (George Burns) friend Tracy (Louanne) should be expelled from school and sent to a mental institution due to the girl's claim to have personally seen and talked with God. It was also seen as the Internal Revenue Service Building in Washington, D.C., the site of the first job Donna Mills took after graduating from college in the 1991 TV movie *Runaway Father*.

The United States Government District Court Building and the intersection of Aliso Street and Main Street are east of the Pasadena Freeway (110) and south of the Hollywood Freeway (101).

The intersection of 8th Street and Hill Street is east of the Harbor Freeway (110) and north of the Santa Monica Freeway (10).

Thomas Brothers Map reference: page 44 at D2 (U.S. District Court Building and the intersection of Aliso Street and Main Street). 1992 revised edition: page 634 at G3; page 44 at C4 (the intersection of 8th Street and Hill Street); 1992 revised edition: page 634 at E5.

Top: The Main Street entrance to the U.S. Government District Court Building seen in *The War of the Worlds* (1953), *Oh, God! Book II* (1980) and in the TV movie *Runaway Father* (1991). (Photo taken in 1990.) *Bottom:* The intersection on Main Street and Aliso Street seen as U.S. Government vehicles approached the nearby U.S. Government District Court Building in *The War of the Worlds.* (Photo taken in 1990.)

An office building at 760 S. Hill Street seen in *The War of the Worlds*. (Photo taken in 1990.)

The Broadway Building at 830 S. Hill Street seen in *The War of the Worlds* (1953) and *Safety Last* (1923). (Photo taken in 1990.)

The Way We Were (1973)

Director Sydney Pollack coaxed outstanding performances from stars Robert Redford and Barbra Streisand for a nostalgic journey from the 1930s to the 1950s, including those sad and exciting years of World War II.

As mentioned earlier in this book, the Union Station replaced the Santa Fe Railroad Station as the main passenger terminal for the Los Angeles area. Dedicated on May 3, 1939, its architecture has been called typical Californian. This atmosphere is exactly what Pollack sought for World War II authenticity.

Streisand received an Academy Award nomination for Best Actress and Harry Stradling, Jr., a nomination for Cinematography.

Scenes for the motion pictures *Union Station* (1950), *Gable and Lombard* (1975), *Under the Rainbow* (1981), *In the Mood* (1987) and for *Oh, God! Book II* as the location where a runaway kid (Louanne) meets God (George Burns) to have a long talk before He takes her home to her parents (Suzanne Pleshette and David Birney). The television movie *Private Eye* (1987) and the television series *Shell Game* (1987) were also filmed here as were "coming home" scenes for the 1991 television series *Homefront*, an ongoing saga of the affairs and traumas of families in the postwar Midwest in 1945.

The Union Station is #101 in the city's Historical Cultural Monument listing.

The station complex including the railroad terminal is located at 800 N. Alameda Street, north of the Hollywood Freeway (101) in downtown Los Angeles.

*Thomas Brothers Map reference: page 44 at E2. **1992 revised edition:** page 634 at G3.*

The Alameda Street entrance to the Los Angeles Union Station. (Photo taken in 1990.)

The station's central waiting area, a location seen in *The Way We Were* (1973), *Gable and Lombard* (1975), and *Oh, God! Book II* (1980). (Photo taken in 1988.)

The station's entrance to the train area seen in *Under the Rainbow* (1981) and *In the Mood* (1987) as well as in television's *Private Eye* (1987) and 1991's *Homefront*. (Photo taken in 1988.)

The passenger loading/unloading area seen in *Homefront*. (Photo taken in 1988.)

Who Framed Roger Rabbit (1988)

This motion picture location must, in my opinion, go down in history as one of the most disguised locations ever built, then dismantled. The location is on the west side of Hope Street, between 11th Street and 12th Street, just south of the downtown area of Los Angeles. Getting there is no problem. Recognizing any of the buildings there that were seen in the film is virtually impossible.

The reason for this "problem" is that the production company wanted to recreate a 1940s Los Angeles, complete with streetcars, streetcar tracks running down the middle of the street, tall palm trees and, of course, buildings representing that era. Believe it or not, the production company obtained permission to close the street to traffic, then actually laid streetcar tracks on the street and resurfaced the street. To complete the illusion, *all* existing buildings were restyled with elegant 1940s façades, and *all* trees lining the street were dug up and replaced with tall palm trees.

If you look closely, one building I photographed in 1990 (page 81) can be seen in the photograph taken during production (page 82). It is immediately left of the El Rey sign.

Then, as soon as the filming at this site was completed, the production company team swooped into the area and restored it to its 1980s look which included digging up the palm trees and replacing them with the trees dug up prior to filming. An enormous effort, no matter how one looks at it.

Photographs on page 82 and page 83 taken during production depict the major "overhaul" this area underwent for filming.

The film's plot centers on a flesh-and-blood detective (Bob Hoskins) who takes on a case of murder involving a rabbit who's animated. This is an innovative approach to a murder mystery for sure.

The film site is east of the Harbor Freeway (110) and north of the Santa Monica Freeway (10).

Thomas Brothers Map reference: page 44 at C4. 1992 revised edition: page 634 at D5.

Top: Hope Street, looking north from 12th Street toward downtown Los Angeles. The site of a primary segment of *Who Framed Roger Rabbit* (now totally returned to its original appearance) is on the left (west) side of the street. (Photo taken in 1990.) *Bottom:* A Hope Street building seen in *Who Framed Roger Rabbit* was next to the "El Rey Theater" in the film. (Photo taken in 1990.)

Photographs of Hope Street in Los Angeles that was transformed into a 1940s street for the motion picture *Who Framed Roger Rabbit*. (Photos taken during production in 1988 by Rich Rosenberg.)

The *Who Framed Roger Rabbit* production crew filming an approaching Los Angeles "Red Car" trolley. (Photo taken during production in 1988 by Rich Rosenberg.)

Hollywood

Alex in Wonderland (1970)

Scenes from this film were shot in Hollywood, along the 6600 block of Hollywood Boulevard.

Donald Sutherland portrays a young film director situated in the film capital of the world. The plot centers on Sutherland and his wife (Ellen Burstyn) and their everyday life as they attempt, against all odds, to be successful in an industry where success is often elusive.

This location is west of the Hollywood Freeway (101).

*Thomas Brothers Map reference: page 34 at C3. **1992 revised edition:** page 593 at E4.*

The 6600 block of Hollywood Boulevard, looking west from Hudson Avenue, seen in *Alex in Wonderland*.

Annie Hall (1977)

This film is Woody Allen at his best as evidenced by the Academy Award Oscars for Best Picture; Allen as Best Director; Diane Keaton as Best Actress; and Allen and Marshall Brickman for Best Screenplay written directly for the screen. The plot is a very funny and moving autobiography of Allen and Keaton's on-again, off-again romance.

Several scenes were filmed at the restaurant "The Source," located at 8301 Sunset Boulevard, Los Angeles, a restaurant reported to be one of Woody Allen's favorite eateries.

This location is west of the Hollywood Freeway (101).

Thomas Brothers Map reference: page 33 at E3. 1992 revised edition: page 593 at A5.

Hollywood's "The Source Restaurant," 8301 Sunset Boulevard, the location of several meetings of Woody Allen and Diane Keaton in *Annie Hall*. (Photo taken in 1990.)

The Day of the Locust (1975)

This film was based on author Nathanael West's novel of Hollywood and the Hollywood film industry of the 1930s. It received two Academy Award nominations — Burgess Meredith for Best Supporting Actor and Conrad Hall for Cinematography.

A lengthy scene was at a film premier. And where else to have a film premier but at world famous Grauman's (now Mann's) Chinese Theater. This historic building has been seen in numerous films, including the 1937 classic *A Star Is Born* wherein lovely Janet Gaynor arrives in Hollywood seeking film stardom. Her first stop was Grauman's and its famous forecourt where movie star hand and footprints are preserved in cement.

The scene filmed at this location for *The Day of the Locust* was not so joyful, however. In it, Donald Sutherland, frustrated by the nagging of a young boy, catches the boy and stomps him to death.

The theater was also seen in "The Malibu Mystery," a *Father Dowling* mystery.

Grauman's Chinese Theater opened on May 18, 1927, featuring Cecil B. DeMille's epic *King of Kings*. The building is #55 in the city's Historical Cultural Monument listing.

The building is located at 6925 Hollywood Boulevard in Hollywood, west of the Hollywood Freeway (101).

Thomas Brothers Map reference: page 34 at B3. 1992 revised edition: page 593 at D4.

Hollywood's Mann's Chinese Theater (formerly Grauman's) seen in *The Day of the Locust* (1975), *A Star Is Born* (1937) and in television's *Father Dowling*. (Photo taken in 1990.)

Double Indemnity (1944)

Regarded as one of the best detective films of the 1940s, this motion picture was scripted by famed mystery writer Raymond Chandler who based it on the James Cain novel of conspiracy and murder.

An insurance salesman (Fred MacMurray) is talked into helping Barbara Stanwyck kill her husband for a great deal of insurance money. Everything goes as well as a murder can until MacMurray's boss, Edward G. Robinson, begins an in-depth investigation.

MacMurray met Stanwyck several times in a beautiful Spanish-style home on a winding street in the Hollywood Hills.

The house looks virtually the same today as it did in the film, the only "improvement" being a modern garage door that replaced the one seen in the film.

The film was nominated for an Academy Award as was Billy Wilder for Best Director; Stanwyck for Best Actress; Chandler and Wilder who co-authored the screenplay for Best Screenplay; John Seitz for Cinematography and Loren Ryder for Sound Recorder.

The "Double Indemnity" house is located at 6301 Quebec Drive, at the intersection of Quebec Drive and El Contento Drive, north of Franklin Avenue in Hollywood.

Thomas Brothers Map reference: page 34 at C2. 1992 revised edition: page 593 at F2.

This Spanish-style two-story Hollywood Hills house served as the home of Barbara Stanwyck in *Double Indemnity*, the location where Stanwyck and Fred MacMurray plotted a murder. (Photo taken in 1987.)

Universal Studios

Frankenstein and other horror films as well as motion pictures and television series listed in this section were filmed, in part, in the heart of the "European Section" of this complex.

The Mummy's Hand and other horror films as well as motion pictures and television series lsited in this section were partially filmed at the only railroad station in the complex, located just outside of the "European Streets" section.

Psycho and the sequels were filmed at the "Psycho Set" in the complex. The tram ride will take you by all of the locations listed through page 100.

Frankenstein (1931)

Legendary director James Whale brought the Frankenstein legend to the screen in a talking version and the most famous version of the Mary Shelley horror novel. The plot is classic folklore around the world; the location Universal Studios, a quality motion picture studio that has produced films since 1913.

The familiar location within the studio where this film was shot is the "European Streets" section which was constructed in 1931 solely for this immortal classic. It must be noted that this location and other locations in this massive complex can only be reached on a tram ride that regularly takes visitors on tours of the studio grounds and attractions.

Many of the buildings in the European Streets section were used in Universal's "Sherlock Holmes," "Dracula," "Mummy" and "Wolf Man" films of the 1930s and 1940s such as *The Bride of Frankenstein* (1935), *The Wolf Man* (1941), *The Ghost of Frankenstein* (1942), Sherlock Holmes' *The Scarlet Claw* (1944) and *The House of Frankenstein* (1945). The "square" of this area was also a European village seen near the conclusion of *Magnificent Obsession* (1954) that starred the late Rock Hudson, and a medieval village seen in a 1987 *Moonlighting* television episode.

The arch and town square location seen in *Frankenstein* (1931), *The Wolf Man* (1941) and *Magnificent Obsession* (1954). (Photo taken in 1986.)

The cobblestone street and Victorian buildings seen in *Sherlock Holmes and the Secret Weapon* (1942) and *Sherlock Holmes Faces Death* (1944). (Photo taken in 1986.)

The corner shop seen in *The Wolf Man* (1941) and in Sherlock Holmes' *The House of Fear* (1945) and *Terror by Night* (1946). (Photo taken in 1986.)

A cobblestone street and buildings seen in Sherlock Holmes' *The Pearl of Death* (1944). (Photo taken in 1986.)

The buildings and street location seen in *The Ghost of Frankenstein* (1942). (Photo taken in 1986.)

The "tall" buildings seen in *The Ghost of Frankenstein* (1942). (Photo taken in 1986.)

Two buildings and an arch seen in *The Bride of Frankenstein* (1935) and in Sherlock Holmes' *The Scarlet Claw* (1944). (Photo taken in 1986.)

More buildings and an arch seen in *House of Frankenstein* (1945). (Photo taken in 1986.)

Both photographs are of buildings and streets seen in *House of Dracula* (1945) and *Frankenstein Meets the Wolf Man* (1943). (Photos taken in 1986.)

The Mummy's Hand (1940)

Even though this horror film contains much flashback footage from Universal's *The Mummy* (1932), it is not a sequel to that motion picture classic. In reality, this film is the first of four "Mummy" films produced by Universal Studios from 1940 to 1944. The other sequels are: *The Mummy's Tomb* (1942); *The Mummy's Ghost* (1944) and *The Mummy's Curse* (1944).

The majority of scenes for all four films were shot on the huge Universal Studios complex. One particular location familiar to film fans worldwide is a small but ornate railroad station, complete with adjoining railroad tracks.

This building was used in the opening and closing scenes of many film productions requiring "hello's" and "good-bye's," and was seen in this film as well as in *The Mummy's Tomb, Terror by Night* (a 1946 Sherlock Holmes film) and in *Son of Frankenstein* (1939) as "Bahnhof Frankenstein," the Frankenstein railroad station.

The building was also the "Wenton, Vermont" railroad station in the opening and closing scenes of the "Headless Horseman" episode of *Murder, She Wrote* that aired on television nationally the first week of January in 1987.

The Universal Railroad Station is located near the "European Streets" section of the studio complex and can only be reached by a tram ride the studio offers to visitors.

Universal Studio's railroad station seen in *The Mummy's Hand* (1940), *The Mummy's Tomb* (1942), *Son of Frankenstein* (1939) and Sherlock Holmes' *Terror by Night* (1946). (Photos taken in 1986.)

Psycho (1960)

Alfred Hitchcock based this horror story on the novel by Robert Bloch. The motion picture quickly became a Hitchcock classic.

Norman Bates (Anthony Perkins) helps his "mother" run a remote motel. A "troubled" guest (Janet Leigh) checks in and is promptly murdered in a shower scene that is now legendary.

As with the other classic motion picture locations on the Universal Studios lot, the only way to the Bates Mansion and the adjoining Bates Motel is on the tram ride. And when the tram stops next to the motel (the mansion rests on a distant hill), one can feel that Norman Bates is glaring down from one of the many windows of the gloomy-looking mansion.

As a note of interest, the Bates Motel, over three decades old, was opened to house two lucky winners of an unprecedented national contest to promote the motion picture *Psycho III*. The "fortunate ones" spent the night in famous Cabin No. 1. Both survived and spent the following night at the nearby Sheraton Universal Hotel as the guests of Universal Pictures.

Psycho II (1983) and *Psycho III* (1986) were also filmed at this "hallowed" site as was *Bates Motel* (1987), a television motion picture that was a sequel to the three "Psycho" thrillers. Note that *Psycho IV* was filmed at the Universal Studios complex in Florida.

Hitchcock received an Academy Award nomination for Best Director; Leigh for Best Supporting Actress; John L. Russell for Cinematography and Joseph Hurley and Robert Clatworthy for Art Direction.

Universal Studios is located at 100 Universal City Plaza, north of the Hollywood Freeway (101) in Universal City.

*Thomas Brothers Map reference: page 23 at F5. **1992 revised edition:** page 563 at B6.*

The infamous Bates Motel and the equally infamous Bates Mansion seen in the *Psycho* motion picture series. (Photos taken in 1986.)

Hollywood Boulevard (1936)

Reputed to be the most famous intersection in the world, Hollywood and Vine has lived up to its reputation by attracting millions of tourists annually. The tourist influx hit a peak that probably never will be equaled during World War II when men and women serving in various branches of the United States military and men and women from the military branches of Allied nations frequented the intersection just "to be there."

The intersection was in many scenes of this 1936 film. The plot centers on a former movie star (John Halliday) who, in frustration, writes his memoirs for a sleaze magazine—memoirs that greatly affected the lives of his family and friends alike.

The intersection was also very prominent during the opening segment of Ole Olsen and Chic Johnson's *Crazy House* (1943) as a gigantic parade heralding the arrival of the comedy team in Hollywood to do a film at Universal Studios, much to the displeasure of Universal management, headed toward the gates of that world famous institution, and was the location for several scenes of *Another You,* a 1991 Gene Wilder and Richard Pryor comedy.

This location is west of the Hollywood Freeway (101).

*Thomas Brothers Map reference: page 34 at C3. **1992 revised edition: page 593 at F4.***

Looking west on Hollywood Boulevard at Vine Street, the location seen in *Hollywood Boulevard* (1936), *Crazy House* (1943) and *Another You* (1991). (Photo taken in 1990.)

The world famous "Brown Derby Restaurant" located on the northwest corner of the famous intersection. (Photo taken in 1990.)

Invasion of the Body Snatchers (1956)

This science-fiction thriller based on author Jack Finney's "Sleep No More" centers on a myriad of strange pods from outer space who reproduce in the form of established residents of a small community. The film was made on a small budget with a virtually unknown cast and no special effects. The result? A motion picture classic!

Actors Kevin McCarthy and Dana Wynter really got around Los Angeles in this film. Even though the mythical town of Santa Mira was the site of the alien pod invasion, the city of Los Angeles and nearby Sierra Madre were the locations utilized by the Allied Artists Studios production company most frequently.

The film opens as a police car, its siren whining, approaches and stops in front of the "City Emergency Hospital." The door of the police car opens and Dr. Hill (Whit Bissell) emerges and hurries into the hospital through an arched entrance to interview McCarthy who is raving about aliens taking over the earth.

The street the police car raced down was an alley on the back lot of the old Monogram Pictures studio (now KCET Television Studios) in Los Angeles. The hospital was part of the studio complex, and the arched entrance was the "old" entrance to the studio.

This landmark entrance was also seen in *Fright Night* (1985) as the entrance to a television studio where a boy contacts a television horror-movie host to get help in killing a vampire who is the boy's new neighbor. The arch was also the entrance to a Long Beach, California, building in *Blood Ties,* a 1991 television movie about modern-day vampires in Southern California.

Dr. Hill finally calms McCarthy down and McCarthy begins his strange story. The scene then shifts to Santa Mira which was actually the city of Sierra Madre and the town square (actually a triangle) which served as the meeting place for residents (turned aliens) to handle the alien pods. Hero (McCarthy) observes this "ritual" from the second story of a nearby medical building.

Attempting to escape the human/aliens, McCarthy and his friend (Dana Wynter) pretend to be aliens. As they leave the building, Wynter suddenly displays emotion (not the demeanor of an alien) by screaming as a dog wanders into the street and is nearly hit by a passing truck. Sensing that they have been discovered, McCarthy and Wynter run around the corner, down a street, up a flight of stairs, over hills, into a canyon, then finally find a moment of safety in a cave.

The Sierra Madre town square is virtually unchanged today, looking much as it did in 1956. The medical building, however, was razed and replaced with a shopping complex named "Renaissance Plaza." The address is 38 W. Sierra Madre Boulevard.

When McCarthy and Wynter ran around the Sierra Madre corner, they entered Belden Drive, many miles west in the Hollywood Hills, thanks to an expert film cut. They followed Belden Drive to Westshire Drive, then up Westshire Drive to a long flight of stairs, today known as the "Stairway of Escape," in honor of this film.

The stairway—149 steps—begins between 2744 and 2748 Westshire Drive and terminates between 2823 and 2831 Hollyridge Drive at Pelham Place.

McCarthy and Wynter then crossed Hollyridge Drive and ran through a series of hills toward Bronson Canyon where they finally found a place to hide.

The old Monogram Pictures lot (KCET Television Studios) is located at 4401 Sunset Boulevard in Hollywood, east of the Sunset Boulevard offramp of the Hollywood Freeway (101). This location is also #198 in the city's Historical Cultural Monument listing.

The Sierra Madre town square is located at the intersection of Sierra Madre Boulevard and Baldwin Avenue, north of the Foothill Freeway (210), in Sierra Madre.

The Hollywood Hills location begins at the intersection of Belden Drive and Beachwood Drive, north of Franklin Avenue and the Hollywood Freeway (101) in Hollywood.

Thomas Brothers Map reference: page 35 at A3 (Monogram Pictures lot). 1992 revised edition: page 594 at B4; page 28 at C2 (Sierra Madre); 1992 revised edition: page 567 at A2; page 34 at D1 (Hollywood Hills); 1992 revised edition: page 593 at G1.

Top: An alley of the KCET Television Studios back lot seen in *Invasion of the Body Snatchers* as the street passing the entrance to the "City Emergency Hospital" as the film opens. (Photo taken in 1989.) *Bottom:* The entryway to the "City Emergency Hospital" seen in the film is the KCET entrance to the "old" Monogram Studios building. (Photo taken in 1989.)

The entrance to the "old" Monogram Studios building on the back lot of KCET Television Studios seen in *Invasion of the Body Snatchers* (1956), *Fright Night* (1985) and *Blood Ties* (1991). (Photo taken in 1989.)

An opposite view of the "old" studio entrance.

Top: The Sierra Madre town square seen in *Invasion of the Body Snatchers* as the location where alien pods were taken from trucks by citizens of the community. (Photo taken in 1988.) *Bottom:* Shops next to Renaissance Plaza (the site of the film's medical building) seen in the film as McCarthy and Wynter exit the medical building. (Photo taken in 1986.)

Top: The Westshire Drive location seen in *Invasion of the Body Snatchers* as McCarthy and Wynter ran from pursuing citizens. (Photo taken in 1986.) *Bottom:* A view of Westshire Drive (center of photograph) from the top of the stairway on Hollyridge Drive seen in the film as the pursuing citizens came nearer to McCarthy and Wynter. (Photo taken in 1986.)

Top: The Westshire Drive stairway seen in *Invasion of the Body Snatchers* as McCarthy and Wynter scramble up it toward Hollyridge Drive in a desperate bid for freedom. (Photo taken in 1986.) *Bottom:* The top of the same stairway on Hollyridge Drive, the location where McCarthy and Wynter rest for a moment before hurrying into nearby Bronson Canyon. (Photo taken in 1986.)

The Jack London House

I include this old house in this book due to its significant place in Hollywood history. In fact, not many persons know of its existence, including the citizens of Los Angeles and Hollywood as well. One reason is that it is situated in an alley-like, narrow street (La Vista Court) and not on the traditional neighborhood street most Americans are accustomed to.

Did Jack London actually live in or at least stay in this house? Legend says "yes." Reality says "no." When one approaches the building the first object to catch the eye is a cast plaster bas-relief of the world famous author near the entrance. Above, ships lanterns adorn an obvious barn door. Rumor has prevailed that the building was constructed around 1870 and that in 1906 London came here and stayed with friends while buying livestock for his Glen Ellen Ranch in the Valley of the Moon some 50 miles north of San Francisco. At least that's one rumor.

Another rumor is that the building was constructed in 1920 by a friend of London and that London never spent one minute in the house due to the fact that he committed suicide in 1916 at the age of 40.

Many motion picture scenes, however, were filmed in front of the house on McDougall's Lane (the original name of La Vista Court) as the famous Keystone Kops frolicked. Please refer to page 112.

Did Jack London actually stay at this house? Come, pay a personal visit, observe, then decide for yourself.

As this location is very difficult to find, I provide the following precise directions. La Vista Court (McDougall's Lane) is located between Melrose Avenue and Beverly Boulevard. You can enter the lane *only* from Van Ness Avenue. Van Ness Avenue is west of the Hollywood Freeway (101). When you arrive at this location, you will immediately recognize the "Jack London" house.

Thomas Brothers Map reference: page 34 at D5. 1992 revised edition: page 593 at G7.

The entrance to the famous "Jack London House." (Photo taken in 1989.)

The upper levels of the "Jack London House." (Photo taken in 1989.)

The Keystone Kops' Pond (Site)

La Vista Court, east of Van Ness Avenue, between Melrose Avenue and Beverly Boulevard, not only is the location of the Jack London House, but was the site of many famous Keystone Kops car chases prior to, during and following World War I. In those years, La Vista Court was called McDougall's Lane. The lane sloped gradually from Van Ness Avenue to its terminus where a small pond was located. This is the pond where the Keystone Kops, police car and all, generally ended up after a lengthy chase scene. The Kops' chases prior to ending up in the pond were generally on nearby Larchmont Boulevard. Please refer to page 113.

The site of the pond is at the east end of La Vista Court, just past the Jack London House.

This location is west of the Hollywood Freeway (101).

Thomas Brothers Map reference: page 34 at D5. 1992 revised edition: page 593 at G7.

Looking east on La Vista Court from Van Ness Avenue toward the site of the Keystone Kops' "Pond." (Photo taken in 1989.)

The Keystone Kops' Car Chase Street

In the early days of Hollywood motion picture history, Larchmont Boulevard between Melrose Avenue and 3rd Street was used in the majority of Keystone Kops car chases. After a quick film editor's cut, most of these exciting chases ended up in a pond at the end of nearby La Vista Court. Please refer to page 112 for additional information.

This location is west of the Hollywood Freeway (101).

*Thomas Brothers Map reference: page 34 at C6. **1992 revised edition:** page 593 at F7 and page 633 at F1.*

Both photographs are of the Keystone Kops' car chase street taken in 1990.

On Larchmont Boulevard, looking north toward Melrose Avenue.

On Larchmont Boulevard, looking south toward Beverly Boulevard.

King Kong (1933)

Directors Merian C. Cooper and Ernest Schoedsack brought this monster movie of all monster movies to the silver screen in the early days of talking pictures. And the plot scared the daylights out of the young motion picture fans and the older ones alike.

And a simple plot it wasn't. A giant ape is captured on an uncharted island in the South Seas by a group of adventurers led by Robert Armstrong and Bruce Cabot, lured into captivity, in part, by the lovely Fay Wray and brought to the United States to be displayed to a disbelieving public.

Several locations in the Los Angeles area were used by RKO Studios, the most prominent being the famous Bronson Canyon and the equally famous Shrine Auditorium.

Bronson Canyon, a magnificent canyon near Hollywood in the vastness of Griffith Park, began as a rock quarry that supplied early Los Angeles stone for an ever-expanding streetcar network. Thus the reason for the two caves in the canyon that are very familiar to motion picture and television series around the world.

Probably the most famous scene filmed here was in *King Kong*. The canyon's high walls served as a part of the mountain Kong had his hideaway on. Another film that utilized these same canyon walls was the now classic *Union Pacific* (1939). In 1980, a segment of *Alien's Return* was filmed near the caves.

During the 1930s, Mascot Pictures used the canyon regularly for segments of their serials such as: *The Lightning Warrior* (1931), *Mystery Mountain* (1934) and *Shadow of the Eagle* (1932).

The largest of the two caves became world famous as the entrance to the underground kingdom of Murania in the Mascot serial *The Phantom Empire*, the film that launched the lengthy film career of Gene Autry in 1935.

Segments of television's *Batman*, *Bonanza*, *Gunsmoke*, *Have Gun—Will Travel*, *Fantasy Island*, *Outlaws* (1987) and *Starman* (1987) were also filmed here.

The second primary film location was near downtown Los Angeles and across the street from the University of Southern California campus. It is the massive Shrine Auditorium, a New York theater in the film where the first and only curious crowd gathered to see Kong in his initial captive appearance.

This building was also the location of the Democratic National Convention in the motion picture *Sunrise at Campobello* wherein then Governor Franklin D. Roosevelt (Ralph Bellamy) was nominated to lead the party into the 1932 national election.

I must also add that this is the location where Senator John F. Kennedy made a stirring speech en route to his election as the President of the United States in 1960.

Bronson Canyon is located near the north end of Canyon Drive, north of Franklin Avenue in Griffith Park. To reach the canyon one must walk approximately ¼-mile on a narrow dirt road that runs east from Canyon Drive.

The Shrine Auditorium is located at the intersection of Jefferson Boulevard and Royal Street, west of the Harbor Freeway (110).

Thomas Brothers Map reference: page 34 at D1 (Bronson Canyon). **1992 revised edition:** *page 593 at G1; page 44 at A6 (Shrine Auditorium);* **1992 revised edition:** *page 674 at B1.*

Top: Bronson Canyon, the location for segments of *King Kong* (1933), *Union Pacific* (1939), and *Alien's Return* (1980) and many Mascot Pictures serials and television series listed in this section. (Photo taken in 1986.) *Bottom:* The famous entrance to the Underground Kingdom of Murania, seen throughout Gene Autry's 1935 serial, *The Phantom Empire.* (Photo taken in 1986.)

The west entrance to the Shrine Auditorium seen in *King Kong*. This is also the entrance used by Sen. John F. Kennedy. (Photo taken in 1987.)

The auditorium's north entrance used as a location in the film *Sunrise at Campobello*. (Photo taken in 1987.)

A Star Is Born (1937)

Actor Fredric March received an Academy Award nomination for his portrayal of Norman Maine, an alcoholic Hollywood actor who falls in love and marries an aspiring actress (Janet Gaynor). Gaynor also received an Academy Award nomination for Best Actress. March, in later years, considered this film one of his best.

Gaynor, in the role of Esther Blodgett–Vicki Lester, met March for the first time at the world famous Hollywood Bowl where an inebriated March continually disturbed the audience.

Director William Wellman teamed with writer Robert Carson to win an Academy Award for Best Original Story as did W. Howard Greene for Cinematography.

The Hollywood Bowl was also used for scenes in *Hollywood Hotel* (1937), *Three Smart Girls* (1937), and *Xanadu* (1980) as well as for segments of television's *Mannix* and *The Beverly Hillbillies.*

The Hollywood Bowl is located at 2301 N. Highland Avenue, north of Franklin Avenue and west of the Hollywood Freeway (101) in Hollywood.

Thomas Brothers Map reference: page 34 at B2. 1992 revised edition: page 593 at E3.

A Hollywood landmark, the location Norman Maine (Fredric March) first met Esther Blodgett (Janet Gaynor) in *A Star Is Born* (1937). The Hollywood Bowl was also seen in *Hollywood Hotel* (1937), *Three Smart Girls* (1937), *Xanadu* (1980) and television's *Mannix* and *The Beverly Hillbillies.* (Photo taken in 1986.)

Sunset Boulevard (1950)

This Hollywood drama centers on faded silent-film star Norma Desmond (Gloria Swanson) and her butler/chauffeur (Erich von Stroheim) living in the past in a dilapidated mansion on Sunset Boulevard. The plot gets interesting when an impoverished screenwriter (William Holden) is befriended by Desmond and eventually becomes her lover.

Holden, however, first appears in the film dead, floating in the mansion's swimming pool, relating the story in a series of flashbacks. Quite an unusual opening scene.

Before becoming "associated" with Norma Desmond, Holden's character in the film resided in a Spanish colonial apartment building, complete with a tile roof and wrought-iron balconies, in Hollywood. It is the perfect setting for the home of an unemployed screenwriter.

The building selected for this segment of the film was the Alto-Nido apartment building, located at 1851 N. Ivar Avenue, west of Vine Street and north of Yucca Street in Hollywood.

Charles Brackett, Billy Wilder and D.M. Marshman, Jr., received Academy Awards for their story and screenplay.

Academy Award nominations went out for Best Picture; Wilder, Best Director; Holden, Best Actor; Swanson, Best Actress; von Stroheim, Best Supporting Actor; and John F. Seitz, Cinematography.

*Thomas Brothers Map reference: page 34 at C2. **1992 revised edition: page 593 at F4.***

This Spanish colonial apartment building overlooking Sunset Boulevard was the location in *Sunset Boulevard* where William Holden lived before he moved in with Gloria Swanson. (Photo taken in 1987.)

Other Communities

——— Agua Dulce ———

Star Trek (1966 to 1969)

Even though this science fiction television series has the reputation of being on television in first runs for decades, it lasted but three years (September 8, 1966–September 2, 1969). But what a three years as the series made Capt. James T. Kirk (William Shatner) and Mr. Spock (Leonard Nimoy) household names throughout the world.

Although the vast majority of filming for the series episodes was done in the studio, the cast and crew occasionally ventured outside, finding a location that resembled a distant planet. The Vasquez Rocks in Vasquez Park are such a location and served as a remote planet on Episode #17 ("Shore Leave") in October of 1966.

Before I proceed to other motion pictures and television series filmed at this location, allow me to pass on a bit of Star Trek trivia. The present television series *Star Trek: The Next Generation* notwithstanding, *Star Trek* did return to the television screen from 1973 to 1975 in animated form with the original cast members supplying the voices.

The Vasquez Rocks are unique in that a different camera angle easily creates a part of the old west that was seen in scores of Western films such as Rocky Lane's *Bandits of Dark Canyon* (1947), Roy Rogers' *The Far Frontier* (1948) and *The Legend of the Lone Ranger* (1981). The rocks and the park were also seen in the motion picture *The Three Kings* (1987) and in *Sweet Poison* (1991) as a desolate area where an escaped convict (Steven Bauer) kills his partner during the kidnapping of a mismatched couple (Edward Herrmann and Patricia Healy). Segments of *For the Boys* (1991) were also shot here. This film starred Bette Midler and James Caan as entertainers in the United Service Organization (USO), the fabled and talented group of individuals who provided entertainment for American servicemen and women in peacetime and during the dark days of war.

This park is also a favorite location for television production companies. Segments of television's *Hell Town* that starred Robert Blake where shot here as were two segments of *Fantasy Island,* one as a prehistoric earth setting and once for a Bigfoot locale.

Perhaps the most famous scene shot at this location was for the motion picture *Marilyn: The Untold Story* (1980). This is due to the enormous popularity of the late actress, a popularity that grows as each year passes. It is to be expected, then, that her many fans continually seek out anything connected with her, either personally or professionally, including motion picture locations where other actresses appeared to portray her.

In this film based on author Norman Mailer's best-seller, Catherine Hicks appears as Monroe. Early in the film, Monroe gets a break, of sorts, and is offered a photo session. She eagerly accepts. This now famous session, according to Monroe lore, launched her on the way to superstardom.

Vasquez Rocks Park is located north of the Antelope Valley Freeway (14), at the intersection of Schaefer Road and Agua Dulce Canyon Road in the city of Agua Dulce.

Thomas Brothers Map reference: page 188 at C2. 1992 revised edition: page 4463 at E2.

Top: The park's "mountain" on an alien planet seen in a *Star Trek* TV episode, as Big Foot's home on a *Fantasy Island* TV episode, as the location of Marilyn Monroe's photo session in *Marilyn: The Untold Story* (1980) and other films mentioned in this section. (Photo taken in 1988.) *Bottom:* A cliff on an alien planet seen in a *Star Trek* television episode. (Photo taken in 1986.)

Western badlands (top photo) and a stagecoach trail (bottom photo) seen in the Western films listed in this section. (Photos taken in 1986.)

———————— Arcadia ————————

Fantasy Island (1977)

Often referred to as the "Father" of the popular television series of the same name, this film is often compared to *Westworld* (1973) and that film's sequel, *Futureworld* (1973). All have the same basic plot; an expensive vacation with all wishes fulfilled.

On *Fantasy Island,* mysterious millionaire Mr. Roarke's (Ricardo Montalban) island paradise, any guest with $50,000 can live out any fantasy. The immense popularity of this film spawned the television series that was first telecast on January 28, 1978, and ended its long run on August 18, 1984.

In the opening of each television episode, a very small person by the name of Tattoo (Herve Villechaize) climbed the tower of a lovely old house and rang a large bell to announce the arrival of a seaplane carrying guests. Note: Villechaize was replaced in 1983 by robust actor Christopher Hewett who never climbed the steep, narrow steps of the tower. Instead, he simply pressed a button that materialized for the 1983 season to cause the bell to ring.

Mr. Roarke's house with the bell tower is located on the vast grounds of the Los Angeles State and County Arboretum, a location that is regularly used by more motion picture and television series production companies than anywhere else on the earth.

The grounds of the arboretum have provided a setting for over one hundred motion pictures and scores of television specials, series episodes and mini-series since 1937.

The most identifiable landmark on the arboretum grounds is the world famous Queen Anne Cottage (Mr. Roarke's house), located next to the lagoon in the "Historical Area" of the 127-acre complex.

The television series *Fantasy Island* filmed here initially but it must be noted that the Queen Anne Cottage and the lagoon were the principal setting for only the 1977 season as the production company constructed a replica set on their back lot in 1978 as it was more convenient to film at the studio than to go on location with cast, crew and equipment. It was less expensive, too.

It was also less expensive to provide the seaplane that carried the guests to the island each week as an actual seaplane was brought to the arboretum for weekly filming by truck and placed in the water by crane.

Other television series filmed in the arboretum are: *The Love Boat* (1978), *Knots Landing* (1981), *Dallas* (1981), *Hart to Hart* (1982) and *Dynasty* (1984).

Top: **Mr. Roarke's (Ricardo Montalban)** *Fantasy Island* **mansion, the world famous Queen Anne Cottage, seen in the television series. (Photo taken in 1988.)** *Bottom:* **The shoreline of** *Fantasy Island* **where the seaplane landed and unloaded the guests who were escorted to Mr. Roarke's mansion located behind the towering palm trees. (Photo taken in 1988.)**

The bell tower of Mr. Roarke's mansion where "Tattoo" (Herve Villachaize) rang the bell and called out: "De plane, de plane!" as each episode began. (Photo taken in 1988.)

Tarzan Escapes (1936)

This film was the third in the MGM Weissmuller/O'Sullivan series and the most costly to date, primarily due to the extravagant tree-house the couple shared, complete with an elevator run solely on elephant power. It opened at the Capitol Theater in New York City on November 16, 1936, two years after production began.

Many scenes for this motion picture were filmed at the Los Angeles State and County Arboretum in the Prehistoric and Jungle Garden section of the vast complex. This area has dense foliage of every description and, of course,

Tarzan's vines. So popular was this location that four Tarzan motion pictures were filmed here over the years.

To absorb this jungle atmosphere, simply stroll slowly along the garden's jungle paths and let an imagination run wild. It's like stepping back into the past when the Lord of the Apes was in command and wild animals dutifully followed his bidding.

The four Tarzan motion pictures filmed here were *Tarzan Escapes* (1936), *Tarzan and the Amazons* (1944), *Tarzan and the Leopard Woman* (1945) and *Tarzan and the Huntress* (1946). Other classic motion pictures filmed here were: *Devil's Island* (1938), *The Road to Singapore* (1939), *The Man in the Iron Mask* (1939), *Gentleman Jim* (1942) and *Passage to Marseille* (1944).

Now for a bit of Tarzan trivia. Arguments have been going on for decades as to whether Weissmuller really gave the legendary "jungle call." Actually, he didn't. The call first heard in the MGM Tarzan series was a combination of voices of three studio technicians. Later, the call was credited to a film cutter by the name of Tom Held.

The Los Angeles State and County Arboretum is located at 301 N. Baldwin Avenue, south of the Foothill Freeway (210) in Arcadia.

*Thomas Brothers Map reference: page 28 at C4. **1992 revised edition:** page 567 at A5.*

Both the jungle and the lagoon pictured here were seen in *Tarzan Escapes* and the other Tarzan films as well as the motion pictures listed in this section. (Photo of the lagoon taken in 1987, the jungle in 1988.)

Beverly Hills

Beverly Hills Cop (1984)

A streetwise Detroit, Michigan, detective (Eddie Murphy) comes to plush Beverly Hills to track down the killer of a friend. Not exactly fitting in with the somewhat upscale members of the Beverly Hills Police Department upon his arrival at police headquarters, Murphy eventually wins them over by demonstrating "Detroit style" police tactics which are effective in apprehending the killer. Actor Bronson Pinchot who later starred in television's *Perfect Strangers* had a very funny part as a gay art-gallery employee.

The Beverly Hills City Hall was used frequently in this film and in the sequel, *Beverly Hills Cop II,* in 1987.

Daniel Petrie, Jr., received an Academy Award nomination for Best Screenplay written directly for the screen.

Dedicated fans of television's *The Colbys* are aware that the Colby Mansion is actually millionaire Barron Hilton's West Los Angeles home. Few, however, are aware that the magnificent building seen in the opening logo of each program is the Beverly Hills City Hall.

A spinoff of *Dynasty, The Colbys* was first telecast on November 20, 1985. The final episode aired on March 26, 1987. Some of the characters returned to the Dallas mansion, not in Plano, Texas, where the "Dallas Mansion" is actually located, but to a duplicate mansion, complete with a swimming pool, located *inside* Sound Stage #23 on the old MGM lot in Culver City.

The Beverly Hills City Hall is located at 450 N. Crescent Drive, at the intersection of Santa Monica Boulevard in Beverly Hills.

*Thomas Brothers Map reference: page 33 at C6. **1992 revised edition:** page 632 at G1.*

The tower of the Beverly Hills City Hall and the building's entrance seen in *Beverly Hills Cop* (1984) and *Beverly Hills Cop II* (1987). The tower is familiar to the fans of television's *The Colbys*. (Photos taken in 1986.)

Beverly Hills Cop II (1987)

As actor Sylvester Stallone did with his "Rambo" sagas, Eddie Murphy found a character who appealed to audiences worldwide.

In this film, Murphy reprises his 1984 *Beverly Hills Cop* character of a streetwise Detroit detective who returns to Beverly Hills to straighten out the city's elite police department.

One Beverly Hills mansion seen in the film is located at 614 Walden Drive. It is on a shady side street, hardly the ideal locale for a cops-and-bad-guys film.

This location is east of the San Diego Freeway (405).

Thomas Brothers Map reference: page 42 at B1. 1992 revised edition: page 632 at E2.

The Beverly Hills mansion at 614 Walden Drive seen in *Beverly Hills Cop II*. (Photo taken in 1989.)

Busy Bodies (1933)

It's a lovely day as this film begins. Stan Laurel and Oliver Hardy have a steady job at a sawmill and are driving to work, music coming from a phonograph situated under the hood of their Model "T" next to the motor.

This placid scene was filmed on Canon Drive, a beautiful curved street lined with date and Washingtonia palm trees in Beverly Hills, between Carmelita Avenue and Santa Monica Boulevard. Film historians conclude that Laurel and Hardy talked the Hal Roach Studios into filming the scene in Beverly Hills instead of in Culver City close to the studio as both Laurel and Hardy lived nearby.

The happy duo made one stop en route to the sawmill, to change a record on the phonograph. This action took place in front of a house located at 517 North Canon Drive. Odd for Beverly Hills, this lovely old house has changed little since 1933.

The film concluded on the Hal Roach Studios lot where a sawmill had been constructed for the film, complete with a giant band saw that slowly cut Laurel and Hardy's Model "T" in half as they drove away.

This location is east of the San Diego Freeway (405).

Thomas Brothers Map reference: page 33 at B6. 1992 revised edition: page 632 at F1.

The Canon Drive location in Beverly Hills seen in *Busy Bodies* as Laurel and Hardy drove toward a sawmill in distant Culver City. (Photo taken in 1988.)

The house on the west side of Canon Drive (517) where Laurel and Hardy stopped their Model "T" to change a record on the phonograph. (Photo taken in 1988.)

Dark Shadows (1991)

Much to the delight of countless fans of the American Broadcasting Company's "Dark Shadows" series that aired nationally from 1966 to 1971, the Gothic vampire drama returned in 1991 to the television screen, thanks in part to ABC's longtime rival, the National Broadcasting Company.

The first segment of this new version aired on Sunday, January 13, 1991. As 20 years had passed since the original airing, new faces appeared in familiar roles. I was personally disappointed that my favorite actress from the "old" series, Kathryn Leigh Scott, was not in this version as time has been exceptionally kind to her. As she is a personal friend, I can attest to this fact with a clear conscience.

As with the 1966/1971 series, this entry centered on the mysterious happenings that occur at the isolated Collinwood Estate in the state of Maine, located very close to a steep cliff that overlooks an angry seashore.

Collinwood is in reality Greystone, the old Doheny (the Los Angeles oil baron) family estate in Beverly Hills, many miles inland from the ocean and about 3,000 miles from the state of Maine.

The initial 1991 segment utilized just about every square foot of the huge estate which, by the way, is open to the public and easily accessible with ample parking.

The entrance to Collinwood seen regularly throughout the series is actually the rear entrance of Greystone, situated in a spacious courtyard.

An enormous garden area is behind the estate, the entrance being a series of wide cement steps. This stairway was first seen in the opening episode as security guards rushed up it to the garden and Barnabas' first "kill." The stairway was later seen as the play area of young David (Joseph Gordon-Levitt).

The adjoining garden area and its lovely centerpiece, a huge water fountain, was the location of Barnabas' (Ben Cross) encounter with the aforementioned victim, Daphne (Rebecca Staab).

Even a nearby lily pond is seen; it and the surrounding grassy area providing a place of rest for Collinwood guests who try to stay one step ahead of Barnabas.

Forever popular with film producers, the estate was a Louisville, Kentucky, mansion in a 1991 episode of *Murder, She Wrote*, the home of a very wealthy man in the community of Central City in a 1991 episode of *The Flash*, and Stephen's Sanitorium in Chicago, Illinois, in the 1991 "Hardboiled Mystery" episode of *Father Dowling*. Segments of *The Incredible Hulk* were also filmed here.

Not to be outdone, motion picture producers also selected this location for film segments over the decades, the most prominent film being *Forever Amber* (1947), a lengthy film (138 minutes) directed by Otto Preminger and based on another Kathleen Winsor novel about a very ambitious young woman (Linda Darnell) in 17th century England who "found" her way to the coveted court of King Charles II.

Other motion pictures filmed here are: *The Disorderly Orderly* (1964), *The Loved One* (1965), *Stripes* (1981) and *Killer in the Mirror* (1986) to name but a few.

The Greystone Mansion is located at 905 Loma Vista Drive, north of Sunset Boulevard in Beverly Hills, east of the San Diego Freeway (405).

*Thomas Brothers Map reference: page 33 at C4. **1992 revised edition: page 592 at F5.***

The front of Greystone viewed from Loma Vista Drive, seen in television's *Dark Shadows* and in the motion picture *Forever Amber*. (Photo taken in 1986.)

The rear entrance to Greystone is the front entrance to *Dark Shadows'* Collingwood Estate. (Photo taken in 1986.)

The garden's lily pond seen in *Dark Shadows, Forever Amber* and the motion pictures and television series listed in this section. (Photo taken in 1986.)

The stairway leading to the garden, and the garden seen in *Dark Shadows, Forever Amber* and the motion pictures and television series listed in this section. (Photos taken in 1986.)

Down and Out in Beverly Hills (1986)

This social satire takes a swipe at the failings of a family residing in affluent Beverly Hills. A *very* rich couple (Richard Dreyfuss and Bette Midler) become attached to a homeless person (Nick Nolte) who attempts suicide in their lush backyard swimming pool. Nolte, after a thorough cleaning and fresh clothing, develops a knack for solving virtually every family problem that arises.

The Beverly Hills mansion used in this film is located at 802 Bedford Drive. The alley seen in the closing segment of the film is located behind the mansion.

This location is east of the San Diego Freeway (405).

*Thomas Brothers Map reference: page 33 at A6. **1992 revised edition:** page 632 at E1.*

The Beverly Hills mansion at 802 Bedford Drive, the primary film location seen in *Down and Out in Beverly Hills.* (Photo taken in 1989.)

The alley behind the mansion seen throughout the film. (Photo taken in 1989.)

I Love Lucy (1951 to 1961)

The sudden and unexpected death of Lucille Ball on April 26, 1989, shocked not only her family and friends, but the countless "Lucy" fans worldwide. Virtually any person of any age who has access to a television set is familiar with the zany antics of this comedic genius.

The majority of the *I Love Lucy* episodes were filmed in studio. A precious few segments were filmed on location, allowing those who loved Lucy the rare opportunity to visit not only a familiar site, but a site the lovely lady of comedy was actually at, toiling to provide enjoyment for countless fans around the world.

In a 1952 *I Love Lucy* episode, Lucy and Ethel (Vivian Vance) took a "Tanner Gray Line Motor Tour" to see where various motion picture stars lived. One house (in the script) was that of actor Richard Widmark. Lucy and Ethel, much to the relief of a frustrated bus driver (Benny Rubin), exit the bus which quickly drives away, and cross the street, then head for a house whose backyard is protected by a tall block wall. There Lucy decides to scale the wall in order to pick a grapefruit from one of Widmark's trees for a souvenir. And the rest of the plot is television history.

The beautiful house in question was not Richard Widmark's at all. In fact, it was the home of Lucille Ball and her husband, Desi Arnaz. And the block wall Lucy and Ethel approached was the wall protecting the Arnaz home from the curious. The wall Lucy scaled, however, was a prop located at the studio, as was Richard Widmark's backyard.

Lucy and Desi's home is located at 1000 N. Roxbury Drive in Beverly Hills. The location the tour bus stopped at was at the southeast corner of the intersection of Roxbury Drive and Lexington Road, directly south of the Arnaz home. A house located at 919 N. Roxbury Drive was also in the scene. All locations are north of Sunset Boulevard and west of Benedict Canyon Drive and east of the San Diego Freeway (405).

*Thomas Brothers Map reference: page 33 at A5. **1992 revised edition:** page 592 at D7.*

Top: On Roxbury Drive at Lexington Road in Beverly Hills, the location the tour bus stopped and Lucy and Ethel (Vivian Vance) got off to look at actor Richard Widmark's house in a 1952 *I Love Lucy* episode. (Photo taken in 1989.) *Bottom:* Lucy's home, 1000 N. Roxbury Drive, and the home's back wall, both used as film locations where Lucy and Ethel approached Richard Widmark's house in the 1952 *I Love Lucy* episode. (Photo taken in 1989.)

It's a Wonderful Life (1946)

Accepted as only an "average" motion picture by fans and critics alike when first released to the public on December 20, 1946, this Frank Capra classic grows in popularity each year.

The film's plot reflects the struggles of a young couple (James Stewart and Donna Reed) in the small town of Bedford Falls. As teenagers, the two attend Bedford Falls High School. They fall in love and are married. During one very humorous scene, the two are dancing at a reunion at the high school gymnasium and innocently become victims of prankster Carl "Alfalfa" Switzer of Our Gang fame who pushes a button which causes the dance floor (the floor of the basketball court above the school's swimming pool) to slowly open. As a result, Stewart, Reed and just about everyone else present either fall or jump into the pool.

The film received an Academy Award nomination for Best Picture; Capra for Best Director; Stewart for Best Actor; John Aalberg for Sound Recording, and William Hornbeck for Film Editing.

The Bedford Falls High School gymnasium was the Beverly Hills High School gymnasium, a part of a beautiful educational complex that opened in 1928. The gymnasium was completed in 1938, eight years before it was utilized for this film.

Beverly Hills High School is located at 241 S. Moreno Drive, north of Olympic Boulevard near the western boundary of Beverly Hills. The school's gymnasium, however, is not a part of the school building. It is located south of the school building, next to the school's athletic field at the intersection of Lasky Drive and Moreno Drive.

*Thomas Brothers Map reference: page 42 at B2. **1992 revised edition:** page 632 at E3.*

Beverly Hills High School and the school's gymnasium, the site of the Bedford Falls High School dance seen in *It's a Wonderful Life*. (Photos taken in 1988.)

The "Bedford Falls" gymnasium dance floor/swimming pool and the gymnasium area seen in *It's a Wonderful Life*. (Photos taken in 1988.)

Pack Up Your Troubles (1932)

This Laurel and Hardy World War I (The Great War) epic was filmed in 1931 but not released until late in 1932. It was Stan Laurel and Oliver Hardy's second starring feature film, *Pardon Us* (released August 15, 1931) being the first.

Pack Up Your Troubles opens with Laurel and Hardy sitting on a bench in a spacious park reading a newspaper; "WAR DECLARED!" proclaims the bold headline. Soon an army recruiting sergeant (Tom Kennedy) and a group of soldiers enter the park searching for men they can enlist. Seeing the approaching entourage, Laurel and Hardy, not at all anxious to join the fighting forces, feign injuries to fool Kennedy. This guise works for a while but Kennedy catches on and the two comedians are quickly in the U.S. Army.

The Will Rogers Memorial Park—a beautiful 3½ acre area bounded by Sunset Boulevard, Beverly Boulevard and Canon Drive—was used as a location for this lengthy scene. The park still has many landmarks seen in the film. The walkway Kennedy and the soldiers approached Laurel and Hardy on has changed little (only a modern light post and a drinking fountain have been added), and the cement edge of the pond a man with one arm sat on as Kennedy and the soldiers passed is unchanged.

A Beverly Hills landmark, the Beverly Hills Hotel, was seen briefly in the opening scenes of the film. This beautiful complex is located across the street from the park at 9641 West Sunset Boulevard.

As a note of interest, the park opened in 1915 as the Sunset Municipal Park and is the oldest park in Beverly Hills. To honor the former mayor of Beverly Hills, the city elders renamed the park the Will Rogers Memorial Park on July 8, 1952.

*Thomas Brothers Map reference: page 33 at B5. **1992 revised edition: page 592 at E7.***

Top: The location in the park where Laurel and Hardy sat on a bench with the distant Beverly Hills Hotel in the background as *Pack Up Your Troubles* began. (Photo taken in 1984.) *Bottom:* The walkway where the recruiting sergeant and his entourage entered the park and the curb of the pond where the man with one arm sat during filming. (Photo taken in 1984.)

A Star Is Born (1954)

This remake of the 1937 classic film relating to Hollywood's tragic ups and downs has superstar Judy Garland in the Janet Gaynor role and James Mason reprising Fredric March's role as the tragic film star, Norman Maine.

Oddly, both Gaynor and Garland were nominated for Best Actress, and March and Mason were nominated for the Academy's Best Actor, but none of the quartet won the coveted Oscar.

Many Los Angeles locations were utilized in this version. The historic Shrine Auditorium dominated the opening scenes where a "Night of the Stars" benefit was being held. Scores of long limousines arrived at the building much to the delight of hundreds of fans lining the sidewalk waiting to see their favorite stars.

Soon Norman Maine (James Mason) enters the lobby drunk and proceeds to disrupt various acts on the stage. This is the first meeting of Mason and Garland's characters in the film.

Near the end of the film, Mason commits suicide. His funeral is held at a church on a gloomy, rainy day. Garland, grief stricken, emerges from the church and is mobbed by fans, and faints.

The church used in this scene is the Good Shepherd Catholic Church of Beverly Hills. It is located at 505 N. Bedford Drive in Beverly Hills, east of the San Diego Freeway (405).

The Shrine Auditorium is located at the intersection of Jefferson Boulevard and Royal Street, west of the Harbor Freeway (110) and is #139 in the city's Historical Cultural Monument listing.

The building was designed by the noted theater architect G. Albert Landsburgh and completed in January 1926. It currently ranks as one of the largest theaters in the United States, with a seating capacity of 6,700.

*Thomas Brothers Map reference: page 33 at B6 (church). **1992 revised edition:** page 632 at F2; page 44 at A6 (Shrine Auditorium); **1992 revised edition:** page 674 at B1.*

The Shrine Auditorium's Royal Street entrance seen in *A Star Is Born* (1954). (Photo taken in 1988.)

A closer look at the auditorium's entrance seen in *A Star Is Born*. (Photo taken in 1987.)

The Santa Monica Boulevard (east) side of the Good Shepherd Catholic Church seen in *A Star Is Born* as mourners approach the entrance in the rain. (Photo taken in 1989.)

The Santa Monica Boulevard entrance to the church seen in the film as Judy Garland exits after the funeral service. (Photo taken in 1989.)

10 (1979)

This motion picture, without doubt, made actress Bo Derek an international star. The plot centers on Dudley Moore, a Hollywood songwriter who is caught up in a hectic and perpetual pursuit to find happiness. Julie Andrews is cast as Moore's long-time girlfriend and Derek provides the stunning beauty Moore seeks.

Part of this film was shot in Manzanillo, Mexico, both at Manzanillo Bay and at nearby Las Hadas Hotel. I was fortunate enough to visit not only the film site at the beach but the hotel as well, even getting a tour of the facility that included the room where scenes from the film were shot. I include two photographs of these sites taken during that visit.

The "marriage" ceremony between Moore and Derek was filmed much closer to home at the All Saints Episcopal Church, 504 N. Camden Drive (the northwest corner of the intersection of Camden Drive and Santa Monica Boulevard) in Beverly Hills.

This location is east of the San Diego Freeway (405).

Thomas Brothers Map reference: page 33 at B6. 1992 revised edition: page 632 at F1.

Both 1989 photographs are of the Camden Drive side of the All Saints Episcopal Church, a location seen in *10*.

The Las Hadas Hotel, Manzanillo, Mexico, a primary location for the film *10*. (Photo taken in 1985.)

A section of the hotel's Manzanillo Bay, also a primary location for the film *10*. (Photo taken in 1985.)

————— Calabasas —————

Planet of the Apes (1968)

The screenplay for this science-fiction thriller was based on author Pierre Boulle's novel "Monkey Planet" wherein astronauts led by Charlton Heston land on an earth-like planet where apes are the masters and humans the slaves.

This film was so popular that four sequels followed: *Beneath the Planet of the Apes* (1970), *Escape from the Planet of the Apes* (1971), *Conquest of the Planet of the Apes* (1972) and *Battle for the Planet of the Apes* (1973). Two television series also aired: *The Planet of the Apes* (September 13, 1974, to December 27, 1974) and the animated *Beyond the Planet of the Apes* that ran from September 1975 to September 1976.

Much of the outdoor filming for these motion pictures was shot at the Malibu Creek State Park, formerly the 20th Century–Fox Movie Ranch, in Calabasas.

This film location is a good 45 minute drive from Hollywood, but it's worth every mile of the trip as the vast wilderness area that comprises the majority of the acres within the park served as locations for segments of *How Green Was My Valley* (1941), *Butch Cassidy and the Sundance Kid* (1969), *Tora! Tora! Tora!* (1970), the *M*A*S*H* motion picture in 1970 and the television situation comedy of the same name that aired from September 17, 1972, to September 19, 1983, featuring Alan Alda, Mike Farrell and Loretta Swit.

Jerry Goldsmith received an Academy Award nomination for Best Original Score for a motion picture (other than a musical). Morton Haack also received a nomination for Costume Design, and John Chambers received an honorary award for make-up creation, all for their work in the original motion picture *Planet of the Apes*.

The Malibu Creek State Park is located on Las Virgenes Road, south of Mulholland Highway in Calabasas.

Thomas Brothers Map reference: page 107 at E3. 1992 revised edition: page 588 at G5.

The rolling hills of the Malibu Creek State Park, the primary film location for *Planet of the Apes,* the sequels and the motion pictures and television series listed in this section. (Photos taken in 1986.)

—————— Century City ——————

Silent Movie (1976)

This motion picture certainly lives up to its title. It is indeed silent with subtitles. Mel Brooks portrays a motion picture director named Mel Funn who desperately attempts to save a film studio from being taken over by a New York City conglomerate. Dom DeLuise and the late Marty Feldman are Brooks' sidekicks. The film is sprinkled with cameo appearances by Burt Reynolds, Liza Minnelli and Paul Newman.

The motion picture was shot at the 20th Century–Fox Studios in Century City. The main studio gate seen in the film is the "old" Fox Studio gate located at the terminus of Tennessee Street, east of Fox Hills Drive.

This location is north of the Santa Monica Freeway (10).

Thomas Brothers Map reference: page 42 at A3. 1992 revised edition: page 632 at E4.

Top: The "old" entrance to the 20th Century-Fox Studio lot minus the guard shack that was located in the center of the driveway solely as a prop for a segment of *Silent Movie.* (Photo taken in 1989.) *Bottom:* Looking east on Tennessee Street from Fox Hills Drive toward the "old" entrance to the 20th Century-Fox Studio complex. (Photo taken in 1989.)

Culver City

Bacon Grabbers (1929)

A "Bacon Grabber" is a slang term popular in the 1920s that referred to a person who is known today as a repossessor. In this comedy, repossessors Stan Laurel and Oliver Hardy are sent to the home of a very tough man (Edgar Kennedy) to repossess a radio that Kennedy failed to pay for. Kennedy, of course, is not too happy with the sudden and unexpected interruption of his day and resists Laurel and Hardy's forceful actions in every way possible.

Shortly after the film begins, Laurel and Hardy, full of confidence, drive their Model "T" down a busy street toward distant hills and the confrontation with Kennedy. This film location was just across the Culver City city limits, in Los Angeles at the intersection of Venice Boulevard and Bagley Avenue.

The Model "T" approaches Bagley on Venice Boulevard then turns onto Bagley Avenue, passing the "dirty" alley where Our Gang's "Wally" (Wally Albright) found the Gang playing with a horse in the comedy *Honkey Donkey* five years later in 1934.

A two-story building prominent in this scene now houses a carpet company. The address is 9349 Venice Boulevard.

Kennedy's house is located in the Cheviot Hills section of Los Angeles, a very beautiful residential area where many motion pictures have been filmed for decades. And the "Kennedy" house is virtually the same today as it appeared in this film over six decades ago. The address is 10341 Bannockburn Drive.

Additionally, a house seen at the conclusion of this film as Laurel and Hardy attempt to drive away is located across Bannockburn Drive from Kennedy's house, at the corner of Bannockburn Drive and Haddington Drive. The address is 2980 Haddington Drive.

The intersection of Venice Boulevard and Bagley Avenue is south of the Santa Monica Freeway (10). The location of the Kennedy house is north of the Santa Monica Freeway (10).

*Thomas Brothers Map reference: page 42 at C6 (the L.A. intersection). **1992 revised edition**: page 672 at G1; page 42 at B5 (Kennedy's house); **1992 revised edition**: page 632 at E6.*

Top: The intersection of Venice Boulevard and Bagley Avenue and the 2-story building seen as Laurel and Hardy turned their Model "T" onto Bagley Avenue en route to Edgar Kennedy's house in *Bacon Grabbers*. (Photo taken in 1984.) *Bottom:* The goal of Laurel and Hardy in *Bacon Grabbers*, the Kennedy house on Bannockburn Drive. (Photo taken in 1984.)

Top: The house on the corner, across the street from Kennedy's house, seen in *Bacon Grabbers.* The address is 2980 Haddington Drive. (Photo taken in 1984.) *Bottom:* The Bannockburn Drive location next to the house at 2980 Haddington Drive where Laurel and Hardy's Model "T" fell apart in the closing scene of *Bacon Grabbers.* (Photo taken in 1984.)

Big Business (1929)

The "business" Stan Laurel and Oliver Hardy embark on in this Hal Roach short subject is selling Christmas trees. Sales, however, do not go well as the time of the year happens to be July. Undaunted by this minor glitch, the two knock on yet another door, the home of Lyle Tayo, a regular stock actor for the Hal Roach Studios. Tayo becomes increasingly irritated by the pushy sales pitch and turns down the offer.

Rejected, Laurel and Hardy go next door and begin all over again. The person the two are talking to is not seen, but a woman's arm soon appears (probably Lyle Tayo again), a hammer in hand, and Hardy is firmly bonked on the head.

The last stop for this frustrating day is the house of James Finlayson, a longtime nemesis of Laurel and Hardy in many films. Finlayson, too, does not want to buy a Christmas tree in July. His stern refusal leads to a confrontation between the three men which results in the near destruction of Finlayson's house, the trees and plants on the lawn in front of the house and eventually Laurel and Hardy's Model "T" parked at the curb.

A typical California-style duplex was the location of Laurel and Hardy's first stop. The address is 3404/3406 Caroline Avenue in Culver City. The street where the two parked their Model "T" to begin the sale is Jacob Street. The front of the duplex facing Caroline Avenue was the primary film location as it proved to be the site of the two encounters with disgusted customers. The door on the left of the duplex (3404) is where Lyle Tayo rejected the Christmas tree offer. The door on the right (3406) is where Hardy was bonked on the head with a hammer.

James Finlayson's house, the final stop, is located at 10281 Dunleer Drive in the Cheviot Hills section of Los Angeles, near Culver City.

The duplex on Caroline Avenue is virtually the same today as it was in 1929, the exception being a fence around the small side yard facing Jacob Street where Laurel and Hardy parked their Model "T."

After over six decades the house in Cheviot Hills also looks the same, the minor exceptions being a metal cover on a vent above the three windows situated on the right front of the structure, and two decorative cement blocks replacing the eight-square window decoration to the left of the front door that was evident in the film.

The Culver City duplex is located south of the Santa Monica Freeway (10). The Cheviot Hills house is located north of the Santa Monica Freeway (10).

Thomas Brothers Map reference: page 42 at D5 (Culver City duplex). **1992 revised edition:** *page 632 at J7; page 42 at B4 (Los Angeles house);* **1992 revised edition:** *page 632 at F6.*

Top: This Culver City duplex was the first stop for salesmen Laurel and Hardy in *Big Business*. (Photo taken in 1982.) *Bottom:* A close-up of the front porch of the duplex. The door on the left is 3404, the location of Laurel and Hardy's initial rejection. The door on the right, 3406, is where Hardy was bonked on the head. (Photo taken in 1982.)

The Jacob Street location next to the duplex where Laurel and Hardy parked their Model "T" in *Big Business*. (Photo taken in 1982.)

Laurel and Hardy's final stop in the film, the soon-to-be-demolished house of James Finlayson on Dunleer Drive. (Photo taken in 1982.)

Canned Fishing (1938)

Our Gang's Alfalfa (Carl Switzer) spends the night at Spanky's (George McFarland) house, hoping to ditch school the following morning and go fishing with Spanky, Buckwheat (Billie Thomas) and Porky (Eugene Lee). Spanky's mother (Wilma Cox) catches on and quickly plans a shopping trip, leaving Spanky's little brother, Junior (Gary Jasgar) with the two plotters so they can't sneak off with their pals. While mom's away, the usual happens, concluding with the four members of the Gang hurrying from Spanky's house and down an alley toward distant Baldwin Hills, a Culver City/Los Angeles landmark seen in countless motion pictures over the years.

The Culver City house used for the exterior shots of this film is also seen in a segment of the opening logo of the television series "The Little Rascals" that appeared in the Los Angeles area for many years and is still seen occasionally.

Oddly, this quiet, tree-lined neighborhood so close to the old MGM studios where many of the Our Gang films were produced has changed little since 1938. Spanky's house, however, has been remodeled.

The back porch of this house, prominent in the film as a huge cement slab where Spanky and Alfalfa watched Junior, is now enclosed with only the steps seen in the film now visible. A low rock wall that parallels the alley next to Spanky's house and a large wood garage with a series of typical 1930s double doors seen in the film still stand, aged but unchanged. The alley the Gang members used to escape Spanky's house as this film concluded is now heavy with foliage and barely resembles the alley seen in the film.

Spanky's house is located at 9634 Farragut Drive, between Irvine Place and Lafayette Place in Culver City, south of the Santa Monica Freeway (10).

Thomas Brothers Map reference: page 42 at C6. 1992 revised edition: page 672 at H1.

Top: A 1930s-style garage complex across the alley from Spanky's house seen in *Canned Fishing.* (Photo taken in 1985.) *Bottom:* The alley leading from Spanky's house toward the distant Baldwin Hills seen in *Canned Fishing* as Spanky and the Our Gang members ran for their lives as the film ended. (Photo taken in 1985.)

Spanky's Culver City house and a portion of a rock wall seen in *Canned Fishing*. (Photo taken in 1985.)

More of the rock wall and the alley leading to downtown Culver City seen in *Canned Fishing*. (Photo taken in 1985.)

County Hospital (1932)

Where else to begin a Laurel and Hardy comedy other than a hospital? And that's just where Oliver Hardy is in this film, his right leg raised high in a sling supported by a weighted ceiling pulley. He is peacefully recuperating from an accident. But the peace is quickly broken when Stan Laurel decides to pay a visit.

Laurel causes so much trouble in the hospital that Hardy's doctor (Billy Gilbert) demands that Hardy leave the hospital early. Unknown to Hardy and everyone else, except two nurses (May Wallace and Belle Hare), Laurel was accidentally injected by a syringe containing a relaxing drug as he sat in a chair shortly before leaving the hospital.

Hardy, unable to drive due to the huge cast on his leg, allows Laurel to take the wheel. Laurel becomes drowsy as the miles pass and the expected happens as the two zip in and out of Los Angeles traffic, their hectic trek ending with a violent collision between their Model "T" and two streetcars.

This is yet another Hal Roach comedy that began in Culver City and ended in a Los Angeles neighborhood. The County Hospital was the Culver City City Hall, located at 9770 Culver Boulevard. The site of the traffic accident at the conclusion of the film was in front of a building located at 4805 2nd Avenue in Los Angeles. This building is virtually the same today as it was during filming in 1932. A large white house located south of the building is the same today as it was during filming—amazing considering the number of years that have passed. The address of the house is 4905 2nd Avenue.

Two years later the Culver City City Hall was a court building in the Laurel and Hardy comedy *Going Bye-Bye!*, the front of the building prominent in many of the film's opening scenes. In one scene, the movie camera looks southwest down Culver Boulevard toward MGM Studios, preserving on film the neighborhood in motion as it was in 1934, including a row of apartment buildings across Culver Boulevard where the massive Filmland Corporate Center that now houses MGM Studios stands.

In *Going Bye-Bye!*, Laurel and Hardy are on the side of the law as key witnesses in a murder trial. The killer (Walter Long) is not happy with the testimony the two give as he is sentenced to life behind bars. Becoming enraged as he is being led away, he swears to escape from jail someday and take his revenge on the two "squealers."

Fearful of the threat, Laurel and Hardy quickly decide to leave town. Not having much money for this hastily planned trip, they place an ad in a paper for a rider to help share traveling expenses. The person who answers the ad and the person they decide to take along is no other than Long's girl (Mae Busch) who is trying to get out of town in a hurry.

Laurel and Hardy go to Busch's apartment to help her pack for the trip.

Unknown to all, Long has escaped from jail and is en route to the apartment. The routine packing experience turns to terror as Long finds Laurel and Hardy with Busch and takes his revenge.

Over five decades later, Rick Hunter (Fred Dryer) and his partner, Dee Dee McCall (Stepfanie Kramer) would report to the Culver City City Hall as it was used as a police station during the early run of the television series *Hunter.*

First telecast on September 18, 1984, this police drama was television's answer to Clint Eastwood's "Dirty Harry" character that was one of the biggest motion picture box-office draws of the 1970s and 1980s.

The *Hunter* duo relocated to the larger Parker Center Police Headquarters, home of the world famous Los Angeles Police Department several seasons ago. All exterior shots of Hunter's new home are of this building. Please refer to the *Dragnet* section of this book for additional information.

The Culver City City Hall was a Hollywood police station in "The Celebrity," a 1991 episode of *Matlock,* and distant Parker Center simply a small police station in "The Malibu Mystery," a 1991 *Father Dowling* episode.

The Culver City City Hall and the site of the apartment buildings where the Filmland Corporate Center now stands are located south of the Santa Monica Freeway (10).

The Los Angeles building, house and busy intersection are all located between the Harbor Freeway (110) and the San Diego Freeway (405).

Thomas Brothers Map reference: page 42 at C6 (City Hall & apartments). 1992 revised edition: page 672 at G1; page 51 at D3 (building, house & intersection); 1992 revised edition: page 673 at G4.

Top: The Culver City City Hall seen in *County Hospital* (1932) and *Going Bye-Bye!* (1934) and in television's *Hunter*. (Photo taken in 1988.) *Bottom:* A view from the Culver Boulevard curb in front of the city hall, looking west toward the old MGM Studios in 1982. Note the row of apartment buildings on the opposite side of Culver Boulevard.

The *site* of the apartment buildings across Culver Boulevard from the city hall in 1984.

The same site in 1990.

The Los Angeles house at 4905 2nd Avenue seen at the conclusion of *County Hospital*.
(Photo taken in 1984.)

The Los Angeles building at 4805 2nd Avenue seen in the same segment of the film.
(Photo taken in 1988.)

Both of these 1984 photographs are of the intersection of 2nd Avenue and 48th Street that is seen in the closing segment of *County Hospital*.

Highway to Heaven (1984 to 1990)

Throughout his lengthy career, the late actor Michael Landon was one of the few persons in the television industry who had a hit series followed by a hit series followed by a hit series.

Highway to Heaven began its run on September 19, 1984. Landon was Jonathan Smith, a probationary angel sent to earth to bring love and understanding to those in trouble and in need. His human sidekick was the late actor Victor French.

As with most television series, the production companies found nearby Los Angeles city streets perfect for certain location shots. The surrounding communities were also utilized as film locations; the lovely city of Culver City certainly was no exception.

Culver City is virtually surrounded by Los Angeles. Its 5.6 square miles are packed with cozy residential areas and business districts that maintain the flavor of the 1930s and 1940s. This is one reason motion picture and television series production companies have used this city for countless location shots for decades.

One of the most popular *Highway to Heaven* episodes was filmed in Culver City during 1984 and released at Christmastime of that year. The story, borrowed from Charles Dickens' classic "A Christmas Carol," centers on "Honest Eddie" (Geoffrey Lewis), the owner of a used car lot whose treatment of customers and employees puts Dickens' Scrooge to shame.

The used car lot seen in this episode is actually the used car/leasing area of a new car dealership in downtown Culver City. The film site was in the dealership complex at the southwest corner of Ince Boulevard and Culver Boulevard.

As a note of interest, this film site is across the street (south) of Our Gang's *Lazy Days* film site and across the street (north) of the Culver Studios (now Columbia Studios), the site of the famous "burning of Atlanta" scene of the immortal classic *Gone with the Wind*.

The location of the car dealership is 9099 W. Washington Boulevard, Culver City.

*Thomas Brothers Map reference: page 42 at C6. **1992 revised edition**: page 672 at H1.*

Honest Eddie's used car lot seen in a Christmas episode of *Highway to Heaven*, the used car section of an actual Culver City new car dealership. (Photo taken in 1988.)

Hog Wild (1930)

The Culver City/Los Angeles film location connection happens again in this Laurel and Hardy comedy.

Oliver Hardy's wife (Fay Holderness) demands that he quit loafing and immediately install a radio antenna on the roof of their house. Seeing no other way out, he begins, tools in hand. Stan Laurel soon arrives to lend a helping hand and the chaos begins.

To give added length to Hardy's ladder to allow easy access to the roof, the two place the ladder in the rear seat of Laurel's car (it is a convertible with the top down). As Hardy climbs the ladder, Laurel accidentally releases the vehicle's brake and the convertible takes off, Laurel at the wheel desperately attempting to avoid oncoming traffic.

After an eternity for Hardy, the mad, hectic ordeal in Los Angeles traffic comes to an end with yet another confrontation with two streetcars.

The Culver City location of the Hardys' house was 4177 Madison Avenue. This house no longer exists. Another house rests on the site. However, an apartment building located next door to the Hardys' house still stands as does a 1920s California-style bungalow across the street from the apartment, both of which were seen in several scenes.

The apartment's address is 4181 Madison Avenue. The address of the house across the street from the apartment building is 4170 Madison Avenue.

The hectic car ride ended between two streetcars, oddly, on the campus of the University of Southern California, in the middle of the street in front of the Education and Information Studies Library at 34th Street and Hoover Street in Los Angeles. Please note that this is private property today.

Once an entrance to the campus, Hoover Street is void of streetcar tracks today and is nothing more than a walkway and a parking area for the university students. However, to make sure this location was authentic, I obtained information from a 1903 railway map and verified that the tracks did indeed exist on Hoover Street. I also learned that street names were changed and renumbered during the 1920s and 1930s as 35th Street became 34th Street, 37th Street became 35th Street and nearby Santa Monica Avenue became Exposition Boulevard.

The site of the Hardy's house is south of the Santa Monica Freeway (10) in Culver City. The location of the vehicle accident on the University of Southern California campus is west of the Harbor Freeway (110) in Los Angeles.

*Thomas Brothers Map reference: page 42 at C6 (Hardy's house). **1992 revised edition:** page 672 at G2; page 44 at A6 (traffic accident site); **1992 revised edition:** page 674 at B1.*

The apartment building seen in *Hog Wild*, adjacent to the site of the Hardy house on Madison Avenue. (Photo taken in 1984.)

A Spanish-style house seen in *Hog Wild*, located across the street from the site of the Hardy house. (Photo taken in 1984.)

The Education and Information Studies Library on the University of Southern California campus seen in the closing segment of *Hog Wild*. (Photo taken in 1989.)

Hoover Street on the USC campus, looking south from 34th Street, the location of the wreck at the conclusion of the film. (Photo taken in 1988.)

Jake and the Fatman (1987 to 1992)

During the first season on television (initial telecast on September 26, 1987) and most of the 1988 season, Jake (Joe Penny) and J.L. "Fatman" McCabe (William Conrad) conducted business in the continental United States. The Fatman later moved his offices to Honolulu, Hawaii.

While on the Mainland, former cop and now tough district attorney McCabe and ensemble operated in "a large Southern California city." Well, the "city" was not Los Angeles as most viewers suspected; it was tiny Culver City. Actually it was at the Sony Studios (the old MGM Studio). The "County Courts Building" scene wherein Jake had his offices and where the courts were located is actually the Irving Thalberg Building. It is situated on Grant Avenue near the entrance to the studio complex. The police station seen in the series, oddly, is the opposite side of the same building, facing Culver Boulevard. This section of the building was again a police station in a 1990 episode of *Dallas* and the TV movie *The Operation*. In the *Dallas* episode, a murder suspect (John Larch) came to the building to take a polygraph examination. In *The Operation*, a police lieutenant (John Sactucci) launched a lengthy murder investigation that eventually led to the arrest of the one responsible for the crime (Joe Penny). Please refer to the *Punchline* section of this book for further information.

The *Dallas* production crew returned as the building was once again a Dallas, Texas, police station in a 1991 episode of *Dallas*.

Finally, true to Hollywood filmmaking tradition, the Irving Thalberg Building appeared as itself in the 1981 television movie *Mommie Dearest* that featured Faye Dunaway as actress Joan Crawford.

The studio complex is located at 10202 W. Washington Boulevard in Culver City. The Irving Thalberg Building is located on the south side of Grant Avenue, west of Madison Avenue. The "police station" seen in the motion picture *The Operation* (1990) and television's *Jake and the Fatman* and *Dallas* is the opposite (east) side of the Thalberg Building that faces Culver Boulevard.

Please refer to the *Metro-Goldwyn-Mayer Studios* section of this book for additional information on the studio.

This location is south of the Santa Monica Freeway (10).

Thomas Brothers Map reference: page 42 at C6. **1992 revised edition:** *page 672 at G2.*

The Grant Avenue entrance to the Irving Thalberg Building seen in *Mommie Dearest* (1981) and in television's *Jake and the Fatman*. (Photo taken in 1989.)

The Culver Boulevard entrance to the Irving Thalberg Building seen in *The Operation* (1990) and in television's *Jake and the Fatman* and *Dallas*. (Photo taken in 1989.)

Leave 'Em Laughing (1928)

Stan Laurel's toothache causes so much trouble at night in this film that rooming house neighbors complain until the landlord (Charlie Hall) threatens eviction.

Taking charge of the situation, Oliver Hardy takes Laurel to the dentist the following morning. Laurel panics in the dentist's chair causing Hardy to demonstrate to his friend that he has nothing to worry about.

While Hardy relaxes in the chair, his tooth is pulled in error after he is knocked out with a dose of laughing gas. Furious when awake and realizing what has happened, Hardy forces Laurel to take a whiff of the gas.

The confusion continues outside the dentist's office when the two comedians enter their car and immediately get involved in a traffic accident. All of this seems very funny to the two who can't control their gas-induced laughing. But police officer Edgar Kennedy fails to see the humor and issues Hardy a summons to appear in traffic court.

The street scenes and the site of the traffic accident were filmed on Main Street in downtown Culver City. Many of the buildings seen in this 1928 film still stand today. One building prominent in the traffic accident scene is now occupied by an office supply company. The address is 3839 Main Street. The Culver City Department Store seen in the same scene was demolished years ago. A Bank of America building now occupies the site.

This location is south of the Santa Monica Freeway (10).

*Thomas Brothers Map reference: page 42 at C6. **1992 revised edition:** page 672 at G1.*

The location on Culver City's Main Street seen in *Leave 'Em Laughing* where Laurel and Hardy received the traffic ticket from the angry cop (Edgar Kennedy). (Photo taken in 1982.)

Liberty (1929)

Laurel and Hardy motion pictures, contrary to popular belief, were not all shot in Culver City and the surrounding communities. The buildings, houses and streets of distant Los Angeles were often used. Such is the case with this film as it began in Culver City and ended on top of a skyscraper under construction in downtown Los Angeles.

In prison stripes, Laurel and Hardy plot to escape from a penitentiary with the aid of friends on the outside. They succeed by eluding a guard while on a work party and joining their friends who wait nearby with a fast car and a change of clothing.

The drive from the penitentiary to downtown Culver City is hectic as Laurel and Hardy desperately attempt to get out of the prison garb and into their own clothing while their "friends" look for a place to dump them off.

Out of the car, the two comedians hurry into the confines of an alley as they discover that they have each other's trousers on and a quick change is absolutely necessary. Their luck continues to be bad as a policeman comes by, sees them half unclothed, and gives chase. They run again, finding safety in a parked taxi, only to be rediscovered by a beautiful blonde (Jean Harlow) in a very early film role) and her escort as they attempt to enter the taxi.

Again in-flight and still attempting to exchange trousers, Laurel and Hardy stumble into and to the top of a skyscraper under construction where the film finally concludes.

The building next to the alley and where Jean Harlow and her escort attempted to enter the taxi was the Adams Hotel. The alley where the trouser exchange was attempted was on the east side of the building. The taxi scene was in front of the building. The address was 3896 Main Street. The building was demolished in 1988. The famous alley remains, however.

The skyscraper seen in the film was actually under construction in 1929 when the scenes for the film were shot there. The building is located at 939 S. Broadway in downtown Los Angeles.

The film site was on top of the building, the roof area facing south. The "V" intersection seen far below in the film is Broadway Place, angling from Main Street. The twin church spires seen in the distance in the film were part of the beautiful St. Joseph's Church, erected in 1901. The church was destroyed by fire in the 1980s and replaced by a much smaller St. Joseph's Church. The address is 1200 S. Los Angeles Street, Los Angeles.

As a note of interest, the huge iron framework seen in the distance from the top of the skyscraper in the film remains in place today, bringing back many memories to Laurel and Hardy fans.

The last of a long line of motion pictures filmed at or near the famous Adams Hotel was *Barfly* in 1987, a sordid tale of the romance between an alcoholic writer (Mickey Rourke) and a destitute girlfriend (Fay Dunaway).

I was fortunate to be present during much of the *Barfly* filming and equally fortunate, but very sad, to witness the demolition process the following year. After collecting a few plaster souvenirs, I departed. Upon my return a few weeks later, all traces of the film site, the Adams Hotel and a lot of Laurel and Hardy and motion picture history had disappeared forever, replaced by an asphalt-covered parking lot.

The Culver City alley and the hotel site are south of the Santa Monica Freeway (10).

The Los Angeles skyscraper and the church site are north of the Santa Monica Freeway (10) and east of the Harbor Freeway (110).

*Thomas Brothers Map reference: page 42 at C6 (Alley & hotel site). **1992 revised edition**: page 672 at G1; page 44 at C4 (skyscraper & church site); **1992 revised edition** page 634 at E5 and E6.*

The famous alley where Stan Laurel and Oliver Hardy attempted to change trousers seen in *Liberty*. The brick building is the Adams Hotel. (Photo taken in 1982.)

Another 1982 view of the alley, the Adams Hotel and the adjacent Solar Store which were also seen in *Liberty*.

The alley and the Adams Hotel, minus the Solar Store in 1987.

The alley is all that remained in 1988.

The alley is no more in 1989; a planter is now at the entrance.

The site of the Adams Hotel, looking south from the site of the alley in 1989, now a parking lot. The Culver City Hotel is the distant building.

The Liberty skyscraper, now the 939 Building. The *Liberty* film location was at the dip of the edge of the roof to the left of the "939 BLDG." sign. (Photo taken in 1982.)

The entrance to the Liberty skyscraper at 939 S. Broadway. (Photo taken in 1988.)

The view Laurel and Hardy had in *Liberty* from the top of the skyscraper, looking south toward the Liberty Church. (Photo taken in 1982.)

The beautiful St. Joseph's Church (Liberty Church) in 1982. It is #16 in the city's Historical Cultural Monument listing.

The site of St. Joseph's Church at 12th Street and Los Angeles Street in 1984.

The new St. Joseph's Church at the same location in 1988.

A Nightmare on Elm Street 5: The Dream Child (1989)

Robert Englund returns as the horrid Freddy Krueger. In this entry he enters a high school girl's dreams through her unborn child and the "normal" havoc ensues. The story also touches on the origin of Freddy.

In one of the many dream sequences seen throughout the film, a truck explodes on a downtown street and is disintegrated.

The street is Main Street in downtown Culver City. The scene was shot between Venice Boulevard and Culver Boulevard, the site of many classic Laurel and Hardy comedies. This same location was seen in a 1991 episode of *Dallas* as a Malibu, California, shopping center housing the Shamrock Pawn Broker establishment where Patrick Duffy picked up a suitcase containing a great amount of narcotics. The address on the building in the TV scene was 3812.

This Main Street location is south of the Santa Monica Freeway (10).

Thomas Brothers Map reference: page 42 at C6. 1992 revised edition: page 672 at G1.

Culver City's Main Street, looking west from Culver Boulevard, a location seen in *A Nightmare on Elm Street 5: The Dream Child.* (Photo taken in 1982.)

Putting Pants on Philip (1927)

In this comedy, Oliver Hardy hurries to the pier to meet the ship carrying nephew Stan Laurel to the United States from Scotland. Laurel, wearing traditional kilts, shocks Hardy who tries to ignore him by having him stay several paces behind as they walk down a sidewalk. A man wearing a "skirt" also shocks curious men and women in the neighborhood, forcing Hardy to take Laurel to the local tailor shop to be fitted for a pair of trousers. The tailor (Harvey Clark) finds that this will not be an easy task as Laurel staunchly resists any effort to have his waist and legs measured.

The majority of the scenes not filmed at the Hal Roach Studios a few blocks down the street were shot on Main Street, near Culver Boulevard, in Culver City at or near the historic Culver City Hotel which is a prominent Culver City landmark. The address of the hotel is 9501 Culver Boulevard. The entrance, however, is on Main Street and was seen in several scenes. It has been modified somewhat over the decades but looks much the same today as it did in 1927 during filming.

The location where Hardy ignored Laurel on the sidewalk was just south of the hotel on the east side of Culver Boulevard. I took several photographs of this location in 1983 as the demolition of all buildings on the east side of the boulevard began. A Spanish-style apartment complex now occupies this important film location.

Over 50 years later, in 1981, segments for *Under the Rainbow* were shot at the Culver City Hotel. The stars of *Under the Rainbow* were Chevy Chase and Carrie Fisher. The film, a comedy, revolved around the many problems caused by the "Little People" hired by MGM Studios in 1939 to appear as Munchkins in the color extravaganza, *The Wizard of Oz*.

The Little People were housed at the hotel in this film which was loosely based on a true incident. In reality, the MGM Studios arranged for accommodations for the Little People and others who appeared in the film at the hotel simply because it was so close to the studio.

Erected in 1924, the Culver City Hotel is not only a city landmark, but a motion picture landmark seen in countless silent films and comedies over the decades. Of late, television's *Sledge Hammer!* and a Christmas episode of *Highway to Heaven* were filmed near the stately old building.

The Culver City Hotel is south of the Santa Monica Freeway (10).

*Thomas Brothers Map reference: page 42 at C6. **1992 revised edition: page 672 at G1.***

Top: The Main Street entrance to the Culver City Hotel at Washington Boulevard. The Adams Hotel (now demolished) is across Main Street in this 1986 photograph. *Bottom:* A close-up view of the hotel's Main Street entrance seen in *Putting Pants on Philip* and in television's *Sledge Hammer!* and *Highway to Heaven.* (Photo taken in 1987.)

Both photographs are of the east side of Culver Boulevard, south of the Culver City Hotel, seen in *Putting Pants on Philip*. (Photos taken in 1983.)

The Spanish-style apartment complex that replaced the row of buildings on the east side of Culver Boulevard seen in *Putting Pants on Philip*. (Center of photograph.) (Photo taken in 1988.)

Small Talk (1929)

In this first "talking" Our Gang film, the members of the Gang are cast as orphans hoping for adoption. Wheezer (Bobby Hutchins) and Mary Ann (Mary Ann Jackson) are brother and sister. Wheezer is finally adopted by a rich socialite (Helen Jerome Eddy) and taken to live in the family mansion. Mary Ann and the rest of the Gang decide to go to the mansion, break in and visit Wheezer. They do so, and while in the mansion, Mary Ann and her friend, Gang member Jean Darling, accidentally set off a fire and police alarm that causes a herd of public servants to hurry to the mansion, much to the dismay of Wheezer's new parents.

The mansion was located in the studio. The street in front of the mansion where the emergency vehicles arrived in response to the emergency alarm was Lafayette Place in Culver City. The row of houses with chimneys that faced the mansion are located at 4052 Lafayette Place. The fire and police vehicles all came from around the corner from Fire Department Number 1, an actual fire station located next to the Culver City City Hall. The address of the fire station is 9760 Culver Boulevard.

All locations are south of the Santa Monica Freeway (10).

Thomas Brothers Map reference: page 42 at C6. 1992 revised edition: page 672 at G1.

Top: The row of houses seen in *Small Talk*, across Lafayette Place from the studio site of Wheezer's house. (Photo taken in 1988.) *Bottom:* The fire station on Culver Boulevard seen in *Small Talk* as the fire engines began their run to Wheezer's house. Note the Culver City Hotel in the distance. (Photo taken in 1988.)

Two Tars (1928)

Dressed in the uniform of the U.S. Navy, sailors Stan Laurel and Oliver Hardy begin this film by coming to town after a stint at sea. With money to spend, they rent a car and immediately bang into a streetlight pole. After a brief argument, the two continue down the busy street and spot two lovely young ladies (Thelma Hill and Ruby Blaine). They promptly introduce themselves and offer them a ride in the country.

Away from downtown Culver City, Laurel and Hardy and their companions find the open spaces open but for a brief time as they soon get stuck in a horrid traffic jam. Eager to escape this congestion, Hardy backs the car and bangs into the car behind. The car's driver is infuriated and begins a fight with Laurel and Hardy that quickly spreads to other drivers who are also frustrated with the congestion. The massive destruction to virtually all of the cars in the traffic jam remains one of the all-time classic comedy scenes in motion picture history.

The location where Laurel and Hardy picked up the young ladies was in front of a building located at 3815 S. Main Street in downtown Culver City, south of the Santa Monica Freeway (10).

The location of the massive traffic jam was on the east side of Centinela Avenue, south of the Santa Monica Airport in Los Angeles, south of the Santa Monica Freeway (10).

Thomas Brothers Map reference: page 42 at C6 (downtown Culver City). 1992 revised edition: page 672 at G1; page 49 at E1 (traffic jam); 1992 revised edition: page 672 at B2.

The location on Culver City's Main Street where Laurel and Hardy met the two young ladies in *Two Tars*. (Photo taken in 1982.)

The location of the country road traffic jam and fight seen near the conclusion of *Two Tars*. (Photo taken in 1982.)

We Faw Down (1928)

Stan Laurel and Oliver Hardy slip out on their wives (Bess Flowers and Vivien Oakland) to go to a poker game. En route they see two ladies (Kay Deslys and Vera White). A sudden gust of wind causes Deslys to lose her hat which lands in the street and skids under a parked car. Always the gentlemen, Laurel and Hardy crawl under the car to retrieve the hat. Then, in typical Hal Roach comedy fashion, the car moves away and a street cleaning truck rolls by, dousing the two with water. Obviously feeling guilty about this horrid situation, the ladies invite Laurel and Hardy to their apartment to "dry off."

Laurel and Hardy's wives become suspicious of the whereabouts of their often wayward husbands and go hunting. In the meantime, as Laurel and Hardy dry their clothing in the apartment, the boyfriend of one of the ladies arrives and immediately gets the wrong idea.

Laurel and Hardy have no other choice but to make a hasty exit through a window. Oddly, their wives are passing the apartment building at this exact moment, shotguns in hand, and begin firing away. The sound of rapid shotgun blasts causes many men clutching assorted pieces of clothing to leap from most of the windows in the apartment and flee for their lives.

Obviously keeping a great comedy scene in mind, Hal Roach reworked this scene and used it again as the closing scene in the Laurel and Hardy feature film *Block-Heads* ten years later.

Hal Roach Studios used two locations very close to each other for the two primary scenes in *We Faw Down*. The location where Laurel and Hardy retrieved the hat and were doused with water was in front of a building located at 3916 Van Buren Place. The building has been remodeled but the high curb and the arched cement catch basin (drain) remain unchanged.

Across the street (Washington Boulevard) and around the corner is the site of the "window exit," the Culver Boulevard side of the Adams Hotel. Its address was 3896 Main Street. This part of both silent and sound motion picture history fell victim to the wrecker's ball during the month of February in 1988.

Both of the above locations are in Culver City, south of the Santa Monica Freeway (10).

*Thomas Brothers Map reference: page 42 at C6. **1992 revised edition:** page 672 at G1.*

The buildings, street and gutter on Van Buren Place, primary film locations in *We Faw Down*. (Photo taken in 1984.)

The Culver Boulevard side of the Adams Hotel and the window (far left) Laurel and Hardy crawled out as *We Faw Down* concluded. (Photo taken in 1987.)

East Los Angeles

The A-Team (1983 to 1987)

From its initial telecast on January 23, 1983, to its finale on June 14, 1987, this adventure series had one thing going for it not many shoot-'em-up adventure series can claim. Of the million or so shots fired each and every hour, not one person was ever killed. And very few were wounded.

The team began as soldiers in Vietnam who were caught by the enemy while on a super-secret mission. After the conclusion of the war they robbed a bank of about one hundred million yen but could not prove they were following orders. So they were locked up by the U.S. government, but they escaped and stayed on the lam, pursued by an Army colonel for most of the series. Along the way, they would attempt to right whatever wrong needed righting.

One locale used in the series from time to time was East 1st Street and the St. Louis Drug Co. building in East Los Angeles. This location is at the intersection of 1st Street and St. Louis Street, east of the Golden State Freeway (5) and south of the San Bernardino Freeway (10).

*Thomas Brothers Map reference: page 45 at A4. **1992 revised edition**: page 635 at A5.*

Looking east on 1st Street from St. Louis Street, a film location seen in segments of television's *The A-Team*. (Photo taken in 1989.)

The intersection of 1st Street and St. Louis Street from a different angle. (Photo taken in 1989.)

Cagney & Lacey (1982 to 1989)

This New York City police drama began on March 25, 1982, as a regular television series. And those who conceived it in 1974 did not have an easy time selling it. In fact, it was turned down by all three networks, finally making the grade as a made-for-television movie in October of 1981.

A female version of *Starsky and Hutch,* it grabbed an immediate following and with some character changes appeared as a series the following year.

The team was Chris Cagney, the single, rather ambitious partner, and Mary Beth Lacey, the wife and mother attempting to exist in the hectic police/criminal atmosphere of a big city.

Cagney lived in an apartment; Lacey in a house in the suburbs. This "New York" house is located at 6521 Pollard Street in East Los Angeles. It is north of the Pasadena Freeway (110) and east of Avenue 64.

*Thomas Brothers Map reference: page 36 at D1. **1992 revised edition: page 595 at E1.***

The "New York" home of *Cagney & Lacey*'s Mary Beth Lacey at 6521 Pollard Street in Los Angeles seen in the television series. (Photo taken in 1990.)

General Hospital (1963 to Present)

This ongoing television serial revolves around the trials and tribulations of everyday life in a very big hospital situated in a very big city. The hospital building regularly seen in the opening and closing logos of this 60-minute program is indeed the "General Hospital" of Los Angeles. At least that was the name of the complex for several decades until the University of Southern California became involved in its administration. The correct name of the facility today is the Los Angeles County/University of Southern California Medical Center.

The stately entrance of the building that faces State Street at 1200 North was seen in early episodes of the series. The part of the building now seen on television screens is the north side, taken from the intersection of Zonal Avenue and State Street.

South of the building, at the intersection of Marengo Street and State Street (on the northeast corner) is the building seen in *The War of the Worlds*. Many sites around the Los Angeles area were seen in this sci-fi classic film and are found elsewhere in this book. Please check the index.

All locations are north of the San Bernardino Freeway (10) and east of the Golden State Freeway (5) on the hospital property in the East Los Angeles section of the city.

Thomas Brothers Map reference: page 45 at A2. 1992 revised edition: page 635 at A3 and B3.

The State Street entrance to "General Hospital," 1200 N. State Street, seen in early episodes of television's *General Hospital*. (Photo taken in 1989.)

The north side of the building (the intersection of Zonal Avenue and State Street) is now seen in *General Hospital*'s opening and closing logos. (Photo taken in 1989.)

A building on the south side of the "General Hospital" grounds, at the intersection of State Street and Marengo Street, seen in *The War of the Worlds* (1953). (Photo taken in 1989.)

Hart to Hart (1979 to 1984)

First telecast on August 25, 1979, this series featured wealthy and stylish supersleuths Jonathan and Jennifer Hart (Robert Wagner and Stefanie Powers) who operated out of their Beverly Hills mansion. Their many adventures took them to virtually every corner of Los Angeles before the last program aired on July 31, 1984.

One memorable scene filmed in 1980 was shot in a massive salvage yard where vehicles of all shapes, sizes and colors come to their end, sometimes with heroes and villains inside. And "the end" is the yard's massive press that quite easily crushes Cadillacs and Volkswagens alike into metal pancakes.

Hardly a month passes without motion picture or television production companies descending on this popular location to capture yet another exciting chase scene that eventually ends in the massive car press.

A segment of *Hunter* was filmed here in 1986 as was a segment of *Simon & Simon* in 1987.

The salvage yard is north of the Macy Street Viaduct, between Mission Boulevard and the Los Angeles River in East Los Angeles.

*Thomas Brothers Map reference: page 44 at F2. **1992 revised edition: page 634 at J3.***

The salvage yard at Macy Street and Mission Boulevard seen in segments of television's *Hart to Hart, Hunter* and *Simon & Simon.* (Photo taken in 1986.)

A view of the salvage yard from the Macy Street Viaduct. (Photo taken in 1986.)

Men O' War (1929)

Naval historians will appreciate Stan Laurel and Oliver Hardy wearing their "dress white" U.S. Navy uniforms in this pre–World War II film. Once a proud part of U.S. Navy history, the uniform was "retired" at the beginning of World War II and replaced by the conventional "whites" we see today.

In this outing, Laurel and Hardy meet two pretty girls (Gloria Greer and Anne Cornwall) on shore leave in a city park. The park's centerpiece is a large lake, complete with a boat dock and canoes for rent.

The happy quartet take to the water and are soon engulfed in a pillow fight (pillows were a compliment of the rental canoes) with virtually every man and woman who rented a canoe that once quiet, peaceful day.

The park seen in this film was Hollenbeck Park in East Los Angeles, just across the Los Angeles River from downtown Los Angeles. Freeway construction several years ago took much of the park property. The lake, however, remains intact and appears the same today as it did in this film. A stone and tile section of the old boathouse connects this time with the hilarious time of Laurel and Hardy's antics at the lake.

The beautiful arched wood bridge that spanned the lake seen in the film was the Sixth Street Wooden Bridge. Completed and dedicated in 1898, it was declared unsafe and removed in 1968. A smaller wood bridge was constructed at the same location at the west end of the lake.

The "old" Sixth Street Wooden Bridge is #54 in the city's Historical Cultural Monument listing.

This location is east of the Santa Ana Freeway (5) where the Santa Ana Freeway blends with the Golden State Freeway (5).

*Thomas Brothers Map reference: page 44 at F4. **1992 revised edition:** page 635 at A5.*

Top: The "new" wood bridge that now stands at the location of the larger wood bridge seen in *Men O' War.* (Photo taken in 1982.) *Bottom:* The walkway and section of the lake seen in *Men O' War* where Laurel and Hardy met the pretty girls. (Photo taken in 1990.)

This stone and tile structure is all that now remains of the boathouse seen in *Men O' War*. (Photo taken in 1988.)

A section of the boat dock seen in *Men O' War*. (Photo taken in 1990.)

——————— Glendale ———————

Sherlock Holmes in Washington (1943)

To millions of Sherlock Holmes fans worldwide, actor Basil Rathbone's portrayal of the fictional detective will never be equaled on film. Many fans also agree that Nigel Bruce, Rathbone's only sidekick in the Universal film series, was the perfect Dr. Watson.

This film was the fifth in the 14-film series that starred Rathbone and Bruce (they also had a cameo appearance as Holmes and Watson in Olsen and Johnson's *Crazy House,* a comedy released by Universal Studios in October of 1943). *Sherlock Holmes in Washington* was released on April 30, 1943, and was the first Rathbone and Bruce film not based on a Sir Arthur Conan Doyle story.

In this entry, Holmes and Watson seek a vital piece of microfilm that found its way to the United States, concealed in the cover of a matchbook. Holmes departs for Washington, D.C., from London, England, en route to Lisbon, Portugal, to make a connection for the overseas flight. The "London Terminal" of "Transatlantic Airways" seen in this segment of the film had a stately palm tree next to the terminal entrance. That's very odd for London, but not for California.

The London Terminal seen in this film was the Grand Central Airport in Glendale. This terminal and the airport complex was also seen in the opening segment of *Hollywood Hotel* (1937) as crooner Dick Powell arrived in Hollywood to appear in films. This is also the location Shirley Temple sang "On the Good Ship Lollipop" on an airplane in *Bright Eyes* (1934).

The airport long ago faded into local history, the property now having become an industrial park. Thankfully, the control tower seen in the films still exists, virtually unchanged from the airport's heyday of the 1930s and 1940s. It now serves as an office complex. Both this control tower and the airport have been erroneously identified as the location of Laurel and Hardy's *The Flying Deuces* (1939). Although the control tower is similar to the one seen in *The Flying Deuces,* it has two sets of windows on each side while the control tower seen in *The Flying Deuces* has but one set.

The control tower seen in *The Flying Deuces* (now demolished) was located many miles west of this airport at the Van Nuys Airport (the "old" Los Angeles Metropolitan Airport). Please refer to *The Flying Deuces* section of this book for further information.

The control tower of the old Grand Central Airport is located at 1310 Air Way, east of the Golden State Freeway (5) in Glendale.

*Thomas Brothers Map reference: page 24 at F2. **1992 revised edition:** page 564 at A2.*

Top: The Grand Central Building, the airport location seen in *Sherlock Holmes in Washington* (1943), *Hollywood Hotel* (1937) and Shirley Temple's *Bright Eyes* (1934). (Photo taken in 1988.) *Bottom:* The opposite side of the building and the parking area, seen in the films as the passenger loading/unloading area near the runway. (Photo taken in 1988.)

Long Beach

The Poseidon Adventure (1972)

A giant tidal wave capsizes a luxury liner loaded with passengers in a party mood. A small group of survivors led by Gene Hackman have no choice but to slowly make their way to the top (actually the bottom) of the huge ship with the slim hope of rescue.

No Hollywood set could possibly provide the authenticity necessary to film such a sea epic. Thus the floating legend the *Queen Mary* was selected.

Just about all of the exterior of this lovely vessel appears in various scenes of this motion picture, from the wood deck to the captain's bridge.

An Academy Award for Best Song was awarded to Al Kasha and Joel Hirschhorn for "The Morning After." A special achievement award (new category) was given to L.B. Abbott and A.D. Flowers for visual effects. Shelley Winters received an Academy Award nomination for Best Supporting Actress and Harold E. Stine a nomination for Cinematography.

Many exterior scenes were filmed on the *Queen Mary* for the motion pictures *Death Cruise* (1974), *The Execution of Private Slovik* (1974), *Under the Rainbow* (1981), *The Last Frontier* (1986), and *Someone to Watch Over Me* (1987) as well as for television's *Nero Wolfe*, *Quincy, M.E.*, and *Murder, She Wrote*.

The *Queen Mary* is permanently docked at Pier "J," south of the Long Beach Freeway (7), at the end of Harbor Scenic Drive.

Thomas Brothers Map reference: page 80A at C5. 1992 revised edition: page 825 at E3.

The magnificent Queen Mary, a permanent resident of the city of Long Beach. Scenes for the *Poseidon Adventure* were shot on the decks and the interior of the ship as were many scenes for the motion pictures listed in this section. (Photos taken in 1988.)

——————— Pasadena ———————

Being There (1979)

The late actor Peter Sellers was nominated for an Academy Award for his portrayal of a "normal" man suddenly pushed into the strange world of wealth and power politics. Though he is totally ignorant of these new surroundings, Sellers' silence is interpreted as brilliance. His co-star, the late Melvyn Douglas, won the coveted Academy Award for Best Supporting Actor.

Many scenes for this film were shot at the beautiful Craven Estate in the city of Pasadena. This city's beautiful homes, mansions and buildings of decades past give the illusion of a community somehow lost in time. This atmosphere is a continual lure to motion picture production companies who come here to become absorbed in an aura of bygone times. Of late, television series production companies have found the community to be perfect for many of their productions.

The motion picture *Memory of Eva Ryker* was filmed here in 1979 as were scenes from television's *Bionic Woman* and *Murder, She Wrote*.

The estate is located at 430 Madeline Avenue, west of Orange Grove Boulevard in Pasadena.

*Thomas Brothers Map reference: page 26 at F6. **1992 revised edition:** page 565 at G7.*

The locations of the Craven Estate seen in *Being There* (1979), *Memory of Eva Ryker* (1979) and in television's *Bionic Woman* and *Murder, She Wrote*. (Photos taken in 1988.)

Eleanor and Franklin: The White House Years (1977)

This sequel to the award-winning 1976 television film *Eleanor and Franklin* which was named Outstanding Special of the Year with Rosemary Murphy winning an Emmy for Best Supporting Actress and Daniel Petrie one for Best Director, reunited most of the original cast. The plot was centered on the lives of Eleanor and Franklin Roosevelt during their 12 years in the White House from 1933 to 1945.

A Pasadena, California, mansion, now the home of the Pasadena Historical Society, was used for exterior filming due to its amazing resemblance to the White House in Washington, D.C., complete with elegant gardens that surround the mansion.

The mansion was used as a motion picture location as far back as 1912 by film pioneer D.W. Griffith. Segments of *The Queen's Necklace* (1912), *Western Life* (1918) and *Being There* (1979) have this building as a backdrop.

Eleanor and Franklin: The White House Years also won awards. It received an Emmy for Outstanding Special and Daniel Petrie repeated as Best Director.

The mansion is located at 470 W. Walnut Street, south of the Foothill Freeway (210) in Pasadena.

Thomas Brothers Map reference: page 26 at F3. 1992 revised edition: page 565 at J4.

This Pasadena mansion and adjoining gardens served as the White House in *Eleanor and Franklin: The White House Years* (1977) and were also seen in *The Queen's Necklace* (1912), *Western Life* (1918) and *Being There* (1979). (Photos taken in 1986.)

The Lou Gehrig Story (1977)

This television movie followed the fabulous baseball career of Lou Gehrig, a sports hero who died on June 2, 1941, of Amytropic Lateral Sclerosis (now known as Lou Gehrig's Disease).

Gehrig's feats on the baseball field are legend, the most fantastic being the 2,130 consecutive season games he played from 1923 to 1939 which is a major league record that will probably never be broken. And so popular is the man today that an autographed baseball bat recently sold for $52,250 and the man's baseball jersey with the famous number 4 for a record $220,000.

This movie follows Gehrig, Babe Ruth, their wives and their Yankee teammates on tours of Japan to play exhibition baseball with Japan's best. And even though Los Angeles has many buildings of Asian architecture, the television producers had to go to nearby Pasadena and its famed Pacific Asia Museum to gain the right atmosphere for a Japanese segment of this movie.

Today, the Asian architecture of this building causes it to stand out as though a jewel in a sea of sand. It is located at 46 N. Los Robles Avenue, north of Colorado Street in Pasadena.

Thomas Brothers Map reference: page 27 at A4. 1992 revised edition: page 565 at J4.

The Pacific Asia Museum building in Pasadena served as a Japanese building in *The Lou Gehrig Story*. (Photo taken in 1986.)

Midway (1976)

The Battle of Midway was a massive sea-air confrontation that took place in the Pacific Ocean near the island of Midway between the military forces of the United States and Japan. The overwhelming United States victory proved to be a major turning point in the Pacific Theater during World War II.

This film faithfully recreates this epic battle while taking the time to tell the viewpoints of military personnel from both sides of the ocean.

The world famous Huntington Library and its adjoining gardens with an Oriental theme were used in several scenes throughout this film. This location was also used for scenes in the motion pictures *At Long Last Love* (1975), *The Bad News Bears Go to Japan* (1978) and *Scavenger Hunt* (1979).

The Huntington Library complex is located at 1151 Oxford Road, south of Orlando Road in the lovely community of San Marino.

Thomas Brothers Map reference: page 27 at D6. 1992 revised edition: page 566 at D7.

The beautiful Huntington Library seen in *Midway* (1976), *At Long Last Love* (1975), *The Bad News Bears Go to Japan* (1978) and *Scavenger Hunt* (1979). (Photos taken in 1986.)

My Wicked, Wicked Ways ... *The Legend of Errol Flynn* (1985)

This motion picture follows the legendary actor's life from his arrival in Hollywood in 1935 to his trouble with an underage girl in 1943. The screenplay was co-written and produced by Flynn's goddaughter, Doris Keating, based on Flynn's lengthy autobiography.

A dashing Australian who gave the world unforgettable performances as Robin Hood, Don Juan and Captain Blood, Flynn (portrayed in this film by actor Duncan Regehr) arrived in "Hollywood" at the Pasadena Railroad Station to begin his quest for fame. In fact, this railroad station quickly became a popular location for many motion picture stars of the 1930s and 1940s to leave and return to the Los Angeles/Hollywood/Beverly Hills area in order to avoid the press and fans who regularly haunted the downtown Los Angeles railroad stations, hoping to get a story or simply an autograph.

This typical Spanish-style building is located near the intersection of Del Mar Boulevard and Arroyo Parkway in Pasadena.

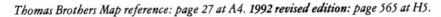

Thomas Brothers Map reference: page 27 at A4. 1992 revised edition: page 565 at H5.

The Pasadena Railroad Station, the location of scenes from *My Wicked, Wicked Ways ... The Legend of Errol Flynn.* (Photo taken in 1986.)

Roman Scandals (1933)

United Artists Studios came up with an outstanding musical for the popular comedian Eddie Cantor. In this romp, Cantor is rendered unconscious and transported back to ancient Rome where he encounters many of the same problems and characters he faced daily in his present-day home town.

The studio used many locations in the greater Los Angeles area to film this comedy classic, one being the Colorado Street Bridge in the city of Pasadena primarily due to its sweeping arches of Roman architecture.

The bridge gained international fame as a result of Cantor racing across it and under it in his horse-drawn chariot. The bridge was also seen in the opening segment of the television movie *Silent Witness* (1985), serving as a bridge in suburban Pittsburgh, Pennsylvania.

Sadly, the bridge gained a dubious reputation as the "Suicide Bridge" in the 1930s due to the many persons taking their own lives by taking a fatal plunge. To date, nearly 100 deaths have occurred at this location.

The Colorado Street Bridge serves Colorado Boulevard, a main traffic artery that bisects the city of Pasadena from east to west. It is located west of Orange Grove Boulevard and immediately south of the Ventura Freeway (134) in Pasadena.

*Thomas Brothers Map reference: page 26 at E4. **1992 revised edition:** page 565 at F5.*

The Roman-style Colorado Street Bridge in Pasadena served as a Roman bridge in the film *Roman Scandals* (1933) and a Pittsburgh, Pennsylvania, bridge in *Silent Witness* (1985). (Photos taken in 1988.)

The Rose Bowl Story (1952)

Monogram Studios produced this rather weak motion picture, the plot revolving around the lives of football players whose solitary goal is to play a championship game in the world-famous Rose Bowl.

This arena is much more than a sports complex; it is a landmark that *is* Pasadena, becoming the center of attraction for the sports world each New Year's Day as it is internationally recognized as the "Granddaddy" of all football bowl games.

The Rose Bowl is also a favorite location for motion picture and television production companies. Segments of the film *Evel Knievel,* a tribute to the world-famous daredevil, were filmed here in 1971 as were segments of television's *The Rookies, S.W.A.T., Cannon* and *The Six Million Dollar Man.*

The Rose Bowl is located at 1001 Rose Bowl Drive, south of the Foothill Freeway (210) in Pasadena.

*Thomas Brothers Map reference: page 26 at E2. **1992 revised edition:** page 565 at F2.*

The Rose Bowl, a world-famous stadium seen in segments of *The Rose Bowl Story* (1952), *Evel Knievel* (1971) and in television's *The Rookies*, *S.W.A.T.*, *Cannon* and *The Six Million Dollar Man*. (Photos taken in 1986.)

───── The San Fernando Valley ─────

Back to the Future II (1989)

This motion picture is the sequel to the 1985 sci-fi comedy hit that starred Michael J. Fox as a teenager who was transported from 1985 back into the 1950s where he seeks out his parents who were teenagers themselves at that time.

In this entry, Fox once again goes on a futuristic adventure, prompted by the strange inventor (Christopher Lloyd) of the 1985 film.

As a point of interest, and obviously to save money, the production company filmed *Back to the Future III* back-to-back with this film.

The Toluca Lake Methodist Church is in the background of a lengthy scene in this film and is also the "St. Ignatius" Catholic Church seen in the 1990 television series *Grand.* It also appeared as a Minnesota church in the 1989 TV movie *Bridesmaids,* the story of four close friends who are reunited in Logansport, Minnesota, to attend the marriage of a family friend. Other scenes from this film were shot in downtown Orange, California, and about the city of Los Angeles. I must add here that as a film critic and the author of motion picture location guidebooks, I've never viewed a motion picture such as *Bridesmaids* that showed so many Los Angeles palm trees in a Midwest setting. One would think that the concerned production company would have made a minimal effort to assure that the background of all scenes corresponded with the locale of the plot.

Note: The original *Back to the Future* (1985) was filmed, in part, at the Whittier High School in Whittier, California. Please refer to the *Back to the Future* section of this book for further information on the film location.

The Toluca Lake Methodist Church is located at 4301 Cahuenga Boulevard in North Hollywood, near Universal Studios, east of the Hollywood Freeway (101) and south of the Ventura Freeway (134).

*Thomas Brothers Map reference: page 23 at F4. **1992 revised edition:** page 563 at B5.*

The Toluca Lake United Methodist Church at 4301 Cahuenga Boulevard, a location seen in *Back to the Future II* (1989) and *Bridesmaids* (1989) as well as in television's *Grand*. (Photo taken in 1989.)

Casablanca (1942)

Considered to be one of the 10 best films ever made, this World War II entry launched actor Humphrey Bogart on his way to becoming a legend in the industry. Although much of the film was shot at Warner Brothers Studios, location filming was done at the Los Angeles Metropolitan Airport which is now the Van Nuys Airport.

The hangar seen in this film still stands but is no longer a part of the airport complex. It was sold many years ago and is now occupied by a shipping company.

The plot of the film was typical World War II. The difference between the "B" film it should have been and the classic it became was the presence of Bogart, Ingrid Bergman, Claude Rains, Paul Henried, Conrad Veidt, S.Z. Sakall, Peter Lorre, and, of course, Dooley Wilson as "Sam."

The result was Academy Awards for Best Picture, Best Director (Michael Curtiz), and Best Screenplay (Julius Epstein, Philip Epstein and Howard Koch). Bogart was nominated for Best Actor, Rains for Best Supporting Actor and Arthur Edeson for Cinematography.

The address of this extremely important part of Hollywood history is

16217 Lindberg Street. The rear of the building is the film location as it was the entrance to the hangar in 1942. This location faces Waterman Drive, a narrow street that borders the realigned airport property. It is on the south side of Waterman Drive, west of Woodley Avenue in the Van Nuys area of Los Angeles. Film buffs will appreciate that Waterman Drive is the site of part of the original runway seen in the film.

As a note of interest, this building is immediately west of the site of the airplane hangar seen in Laurel & Hardy's *The Flying Deuces* (1939) which was also seen briefly in this film. *The Flying Deuces* hangar, sadly, was demolished shortly after I took several photographs of this historic film location. Please refer to *The Flying Deuces* section of this book for further information.

The art deco control tower that *was* a Los Angeles Metropolitan Airport landmark was seen in the opening and closing scenes of *Casablanca*. It was called the "radio tower" in the film. It was also seen in *The Flying Deuces* and in Chapter 9 of the Dead End Kids' serial *Junior G-Men* that was filmed here in 1940.

The Van Nuys Airport is located west of Woodley Avenue, between Roscoe Boulevard and Vanowen Street. The address is 16461 Sherman Way, Van Nuys.

Thomas Brothers Map reference: page 14 at F3 (airport entrance). ***1992 revised edition:*** *page 531 at E5; page 15 at A2 (hangar location);* ***1992 revised edition:*** *page 531 at F3.*

The airplane hangar used for exterior filming for segments of *Casablanca*. (Photo taken in 1986.)

The "old" runway seen in the film, now Waterman Drive, looking west toward the site of the control tower seen in the film. (Photo taken in 1987.)

Dallas (1978 to 1991)

The initial telecast of this drama was on April 2, 1978. The series concluded on May 3, 1991, after 13 years making it second only to *Gunsmoke* as the longest running nightime soap opera in television history.

Even though the majority of the weekly series plots were centered in Dallas, Texas, approximately 90% of the filming was in Los Angeles and Culver City, California. Please refer to the index section of this book for additional sites.

In the next to last episode, filmed April 26, 1991, Vahalla Memorial Park in North Hollywood was a Dallas cemetery where the Susan Lucci character was buried. Bobby Ewing (Patrick Duffy) was the only member of the Ewing clan present to bid a farewell.

Although not used regularly as a film location, Vahalla Memorial Park is world famous as the final resting place of Oliver Hardy, the heavier half of the immortal comedy team of Laurel and Hardy. Hardy's gravesite is a short distance (to the right and behind a wall) from the massive fountain that dominated this *Dallas* scene.

Vahalla Memorial Park is located at 10621 Victory Boulevard, North Hollywood, north of the Ventura Freeway (134).

Thomas Brothers Map reference: page 16 at F5. 1992 revised edition: page 533 at B6.

Vahalla Memorial Park's fountain, a location seen in the next to last (April 26, 1991) episode of television's *Dallas*. (Photo taken in 1982.)

The final resting place of comedic genius Oliver Hardy at Vahalla Memorial Park. (Photo taken in 1988.)

Dynasty (1981 to 1991)

The beautiful Warner Center Marriott Hotel is one of the most-filmed hotels in the city's vast San Fernando Valley. Location managers generally attempt to avoid using a site more than once, especially for a television series. Large hotels, however, are an exception due to the perpetual turnover of guests, which prevents the same old faces from appearing on camera.

The unique architecture of this building allows it to be used as something other than a hotel. The ballroom, for example, was turned into a Las Vegas casino for a *Hunter* episode, and the hotel's rooftop parking area as a heliport for an episode of *J.J. Starbuck*. In the *Dynasty* series, the hotel became a Denver, Colorado, hotel.

Other television series filmed here were: *A Year in the Life, Falcon Crest, Highway to Heaven* and *Matlock*.

The Warner Center Marriott Hotel is located at 21850 Oxnard Street, Woodland Hills, north of the Ventura Freeway (101).

*Thomas Brothers Map reference: page 12 at C6. **1992 revised edition:** page 560 at A1.*

Both 1989 photographs are of the Warner Marriott Hotel in Woodland Hills, seen in *Dynasty, Hunter, J.J. Starbuck* and the other television series listed in this section.

Earth Girls Are Easy (1989)

The Spanish-style, rustic charm of the Olive View Medical Center, located in the San Fernando Valley of Los Angeles, was used for many scenes in this film. And hospital locations are not uncommon in motion picture and/or television series productions as this is a way for hospitals to earn additional money to offset ever-increasing medical costs. A spokesman for the American Hospital Association stated that, in fact, many local hospitals are experiencing financial difficulties and are looking for ways to earn money. The fee of from $3,000 to $5,000 per day motion picture and television production companies pay most medical facilities most certainly helps.

Earth Girls Are Easy is a musical comedy of sorts that stars Geena Davis as a "Valley Girl" who teams up with three space aliens whose space ship crashes into her swimming pool.

Other motion pictures filmed here include *Beverly Hills Cop II* (1987), *Over the Top* (1987) and *The Couch Trip* (1988). Television's *Buck James, The Colbys, Highway to Heaven, Murder, She Wrote, Ohara* and *Simon & Simon* also utilized the site.

Beverly Hills Cop II is the sequel to Eddie Murphy's smash hit of 1984. *Over the Top* stars Sylvester Stallone as a father trying hard to impress his son, and *The Couch Trip* is a Dan Aykroyd/Walter Matthau comedy.

The Olive View Medical Center is located at 14445 Olive View Drive, Sylmar, north of the Foothill Freeway (210) and east of the Golden State Freeway (5).

Thomas Brothers Map reference: page 2 at D1. 1992 revised edition: page 482 at A1.

Both 1989 photographs are of a section of the Olive View Medical Center seen in *Earth Girls Are Easy* (1989), *Beverly Hills Cop II* (1987) and other motion pictures and television series listed in this section.

The Flying Deuces (1939)

In this feature motion picture, Stan Laurel and Oliver Hardy are in Paris, France, where Hardy falls in love with a beautiful waitress (Jean Parker) who has no interest in him. Dejected, Hardy talks Laurel into joining the French Foreign Legion with him so he can "forget."

Although this film has very funny moments, especially the "laundry scene" and the "flying scene," it is a rare Laurel and Hardy entry as one of the comedy duo (Hardy) is killed near the film's conclusion.

The North Africa airport near the Foreign Legion fort where the flying scenes and many chase scenes were filmed was the Los Angeles Metropolitan Airport which is now the Van Nuys Airport. Much has changed since this film was shot there, including the demolition of many sites familiar to Laurel and Hardy fans.

The art deco control tower so prominent in the flying and chase scenes was demolished in the 1960s due to an airport expansion program. The old runway is partially intact immediately west of the site of the control tower. Both of these film locations remain on airport property.

Sadly, the airplane hangar seen in the film was recently demolished. All that now remains is the cement foundation. In its latter years, this hangar was sold to a private party and converted to a machine shop. Its address was 16205 Lindbergh Street. This location is no longer a part of the airport property.

The now classic Laurel and Hardy scenes were filmed at the rear of the building (the hangar's entrance in 1939) which faced the old runway which is now a part of Waterman Drive, a narrow street that borders the realigned airport property. This film site is on the south side of Waterman Drive, west of Woodley Avenue in the Van Nuys area of Los Angeles.

This hangar, the old runway and the art deco control tower were also seen in Chapter 9 of the Dead End Kids' serial *Junior G-Men* (1940) and in the opening and closing scenes of the motion picture classic *Casablanca* (1942). As a note of interest, the Laurel and Hardy hangar site is immediately east of the airplane hangar seen in *Casablanca*. Please refer to the *Casablanca* section of this book for further information.

The classic "laundry scene" was filmed at the famous Iverson Ranch, many miles west of Van Nuys in Chatsworth. In this scene, Laurel and Hardy were assigned to the laundry detail as punishment. And the two were the *only* Legionnaires assigned to this detail and the tons of clothing to be washed in a single day. This scene is memorable due to the seemingly endless lines of white clothing stretching to the horizon and the huge pile of white clothing that increased in size with each truckload dumped on the ground.

Laurel and Hardy soon tire of washing and ironing and decide to leave and return home to America. They accidentally knock a table over, setting a fire that rapidly consumes the clothing.

As with the hangar and art deco control tower at the old Los Angeles Metropolitan Airport, this shrine (to Laurel and Hardy fans) has fallen victim to progress as, sadly, condos now cover the site.

The Van Nuys Airport is located west of Woodley Avenue, between Roscoe Boulevard and Vanowen Street. The address is 16461 Sherman Way, Van Nuys.

The site of *The Flying Deuces* hangar is on the south side of Waterman Drive (east of the *Casablanca* hangar), west of Woodley Avenue.

Both locations are west of the San Diego Freeway (405).

Iverson Ranch is on Santa Susanna Pass Road, west of Topanga Canyon Boulevard in Chatsworth.

Thomas Brothers Map reference: page 14 at F3 (airport entrance). 1992 revised edition: page 531 at E5; page 15 at A2 (hangar location); 1992 revised edition: page 531 at F3; page 6 at B1 (Iverson Ranch); 1992 revised edition: page 499 at J2.

A 1929 photograph of the hangar seen in *The Flying Deuces*. (Photo courtesy of John Underwood.)

The same hangar in 1987, now demolished.

The art deco control tower seen in *The Flying Deuces* (1939), *Casablanca* (1942) and *Junior G-Men* (1940). (Photo taken in the late 1930s, courtesy of John Underwood.)

An aerial view of the "old" Los Angeles Metropolitan Airport seen in *The Flying Deuces* (1939), *Casablanca* (1942) and *Junior G-Men* (1940). The film location (runway, hangars and control tower) is located in the right center of this photograph. (Photo taken in the 1930s, courtesy of John Underwood.)

Both photographs are of the site of the famous laundry scene in Laurel and Hardy's *The Flying Deuces,* located near Indian Head Rock. (Photos taken in 1987.)

Good Morning, Vietnam (1988)

For you film buffs who are convinced that this Robin Williams motion picture was shot entirely in Cambodia as advertised, you're right . . . almost. One scene, however, called for the destruction of a cafe. Since the Cambodian government refused to allow the use of explosives, the production company rushed back to the United States for this *single* shot.

The cafe was constructed on the Newhall Land and Farming Company property (a San Fernando Valley motion picture site that greatly resembles parts of Vietnam) and blown to bits.

The Newhall Land and Farming Company is a massive motion picture set, covering approximately 40,000 acres with virtually every type of earth surface for producers to choose, including small lakes and rivers, even sand dunes. It is regarded as one of the most-filmed locations in the Southern California area.

Other motion pictures filmed here were *The Defiant Ones* (1958), *Flying Misfits* (1976), *The Right Stuff* (1983) and *Eye of the Tiger* (1986) as well as television's *The A-Team, Airwolf, Baa Baa Black Sheep, China Beach, Knight Rider, Little House on the Prairie, MacGyver* and *Vietnam War Stories.*

As a note of interest, *Flying Misfits* was the pilot film for the *Baa Baa Black Sheep* television series.

The Defiant Ones was a 1958 racial drama that starred Tony Curtis and Sidney Poitier as escaped convicts who were chained together, attempting to elude pursuing police officers. Both Curtis and Poitier received Academy Award nominations for Best Actor. Oscars were won by Nathan Douglas and Harold Jacob Smith for Best Story and Screenplay written directly for the screen.

The Right Stuff was a docudrama about the U.S. space program, giving the audience an intimate look into the lives of the astronauts and others involved in the space program. Sam Shepard received an Academy Award nomination for Best Supporting Actor.

Eye of the Tiger, a film of violence, centered on a Vietnam veteran (Gary Busey) who goes after a lawman who framed him and a bunch of motorcycle bums who killed his wife.

Good Morning, Vietnam was the perfect vehicle for Robin Williams. He portrayed a government radio disc jockey with a rapid-fire delivery that appealed to the United States servicemen and women in Vietnam.

This film site is approximately 30 miles from downtown Los Angeles and 1½ miles west of the Golden State Freeway (5), on the south side of Highway 126, in Val Verde.

Thomas Brothers Map reference: page 123 at D7. 1992 revised edition: page 4549 at F2.

The site of the cafe destroyed during the filming of *Good Morning, Vietnam,* just inside the entrance of the property, near the airport runway. (Photo taken in 1989.)

The airport runway seen in *Flying Misfits* (1976) and used throughout the *Baa Baa Black Sheep* television series. (Photo taken in 1989.)

The runway, Quonset hut and barracks buildings seen in *Flying Misfits* (1976), *The Right Stuff* (1983) and in television's *Baa Baa Black Sheep*. (Photo taken in 1989.)

A house used as a primary location in *Eye of the Tiger*, located near the entrance to the property. (Photo taken in 1989.)

Sets used in various scenes of *The Defiant Ones*. (Photo taken in 1989.)

Hopalong Cassidy (1949 to 1951)

Theatrical films of Hopalong Cassidy appeared on New York City television in 1945 and became a regular feature in 1948. These films were edited versions with William Boyd (Hopalong Cassidy) providing narration. They became so popular that Boyd actually went into television production, using the successful "B" film format. His sidekick was character actor Edgar Buchanan. The first telecast of this "new" series was on June 24, 1949. The series lasted until December 23, 1951.

The primary outdoor location for filming was rustic Placerita Canyon in the San Fernando Valley area of Los Angeles. This site was also used in *The Cisco Kid* television series. Throughout this western series, the Kid (Duncan Renaldo) and his trusty sidekick, Pancho (Leo Carrillo) romped through 156 thirty-minute episodes from 1950 to 1956. The cabin near the vehicle parking area was built in 1920 by Frank Walker. Walker, his wife and their 12 children lived there, renting the cabin itself and the adjoining canyon property to motion picture production companies for countless Westerns.

Placerita Canyon is located on Placerita Canyon Road, 1¼ miles east of the Antelope Valley Freeway (14) and north of the Golden State Freeway (5) near the city of Newhall.

Thomas Brothers Map reference: page 127 at J4. 1992 revised edition: page 4641 at G1.

Placerita Canyon's log cabin, near the entrance, seen in television's *Hopalong Cassidy* and *The Cisco Kid*. (Photo taken in 1989.)

An old trail leading back into Placerita Canyon seen in television's *Hopalong Cassidy* and *The Cisco Kid*. (Photo taken in 1989.)

Punchline (1988)

Scenes for this Tom Hanks/Sally Field motion picture were shot at the Lake View Medical Center, a facility one motion picture location manager claims is seen in about 75% of all hospital films.

The motion picture *The Burning Bed* (1984) was also filmed here as were segments of television's *Cagney & Lacey, Dallas, Falcon Crest, Hill Street Blues, Knots Landing, L.A. Law, Remington Steel, St. Elsewhere, Trapper John, M.D.*, and "*V.*"

The Burning Bed related the frustrations of a battered wife (Farrah Fawcett) who, in sheer desperation, sets her husband (Paul LeMat) afire after suffering beatings from him for years.

The medical center was closed in 1986 and now serves only motion picture and television series production companies.

The Lake View Professional Center, an active part of the medical complex, is located next to the Lake View Medical Center building and is also utilized by film production companies. This site was the primary location for the 1990 TV movie *The Operation*. Other scenes for this movie were filmed at Malibu Beach, an exclusive beach community west of Santa Monica, and at the Irving Thalberg Building on the Sony Corporation lot (the old MGM Studio) in Culver City. The Irving Thalberg Building was utilized as a police station. Please refer to the *Jake and the Fatman* section of this book for additional information on this building.

The Operation, a murder mystery with many Hitchcockian plot twists, relates the story of a highly respected surgeon (Joe Penny), who commits murder in a desperate effort to protect his lover (Lisa Hartman) and avoid losing the millions of dollars the two obtained from an insurance company as the result of an insurance scam. The Irving Thalberg Building is the location a police lieutenant (John Sactucci) begins an in-depth investigation that eventually solves the murder and sends Penny into the arms of justice.

The medical center complex is located at 11600 Eldridge Avenue, Lake Terrace, just north of the Foothill Freeway (118) in the San Fernando Valley.

*Thomas Brothers Map reference: page 3 at D6. **1992 revised edition: page 482 at H7.***

Both 1989 photographs are of the Lake View Medical Center (above) and the Lake View Professional Center (below), locations seen in *Punchline* (1988), *The Burning Bed* (1984) and *The Operation* (1990) as well as in the television series listed in this section.

Throw Momma from the Train (1988)

In this comedy, Danny DeVito is cast as a disgruntled son who conspires with a friend (Billy Crystal) to do in his mother, the late Anne Ramsey. One method of execution considered is to take Momma on a train trip then throw her out of the passenger coach door when the train is at full speed. Crystal attempts this but finds himself on the tracks instead of Momma with DeVito waving a fond farewell.

The entire train scene was filmed on the east side of the massive Newhall Land and Farming Company property near the Golden State Freeway (5). The Newhall Land and Farming Company has its own private train at this location, complete with two standing train stations and 4½ miles of track that has been used in many motion pictures.

This location is a little tricky to find. Exit the Golden State Freeway (5) in Castaic Junction at Highway 126. Go west on Highway 126 a very short distance to "The Old Road." Follow The Old Road south a short distance to Henry Mayo Drive. Turn right (west) and you will see the movie location on your left (the south side of Henry Mayo Drive).

Thomas Brothers Map reference: page 123 at F6. 1992 revised edition: page 4459 at J7.

A view (looking east) of the railroad tracks at the "private" railroad film location seen in *Throw Momma from the Train*. A railroad car seen in the film is at the far end of the tracks. (Photo taken in 1989.)

The storage yard at the west end of the property to house the railroad equipment used in the film. (Photo taken in 1989.)

A "studio" railroad station near the east end of the tracks seen in *Throw Momma from the Train*. (Photo taken in 1989.)

A Year in the Life (1987 to 1988)

This family drama is a spin off from the mini-series of the same title. First telecast on August 24, 1987, this new series spanned the lives of three generations of a very large Seattle, Washington, family. The children attended Seattle schools, the teenagers a Seattle high school.

The Los Angeles Valley College, its campus profuse with trees, was the perfect choice for a Pacific Northwest high school.

The series continued through 1987 and the first part of the following year. The last episode aired on April 20, 1988.

The Los Angeles Valley College campus is located at 5800 Fulton Avenue, Van Nuys, north of the Ventura Freeway (101) and east of the San Diego Freeway (405).

*Thomas Brothers Map reference: page 23 at A1. **1992 revised edition:** page 562 at D1.*

Both 1989 photographs are of the Los Angeles Valley College campus in Van Nuys, a Seattle, Washington, high school campus in television's *A Year in the Life*.

San Pedro

Modern Times (1936)

As mentioned in the *Safety Last* section of this book, motion picture historians consider Buster Keaton and Harold Lloyd two of the three geniuses of silent screen comedy (Charlie Chaplin being the other).

Although this film appeared on the silver screen nine years into the sound era, it was considered Charlie Chaplin's last "silent" film even though it contained music, sound effects and limited dialogue. It was, sadly, the last feature Chaplin's Little Tramp character appeared in.

As with most of his films, Chaplin wrote, directed and starred. In this entry he portrays a factory worker who goes berserk, tries to adjust to a variety of odd jobs, then befriends a homeless woman (Paulette Goddard) with whom he falls in love.

Goddard's initial appearance in the film takes place on a seaside dock, crowded with merchant vessels. She is introduced as "A Child of the Waterfront" and then is seen stealing bananas from a basket located on the deck of a boat, tossing some of them to a group of obviously down-and-out youngsters who gladly accept them.

Goddard is finally seen by the boat's owner who gives chase across the decks of several moored boats and onto the dock itself. She eludes the man, however, and leaves the area smiling broadly as she munches on one of the bananas.

The location of this scene exists today, virtually unchanged. It is on Terminal Island in the East San Pedro area of the city of Los Angeles near the city limits of the city of Long Beach.

The scene was filmed on Ways Street, between Cannery Street and Bass Street. Ways Street, in essence, is a long, wide dock. The small harbor seen is Fish Harbor.

Ways Street is east of the Harbor Freeway (110) and south of the Vincent Thomas Bridge.

Thomas Brothers Map reference: page 79 at C3. 1992 revised edition: page 824 at E5.

Ways Street (top photo) and Fish Harbor (bottom photo), the location of actress Paulette Goddard's first scene in *Modern Times*. (Photos taken in 1986.)

——— Santa Monica ———

Inside Daisy Clover (1965)

This routine story of a young girl (Natalie Wood) who rises to film stardom in 1930s Hollywood takes an unusual turn when she marries an established actor (Robert Redford) who abandons her on their wedding night due to his lack of interest in females.

A lengthy segment of this film was shot on the Santa Monica Municipal Pier as the script called for Wood's rundown home she lived in in her teens to be located on a pier overlooking the Pacific Ocean.

A camera angle and a few props easily transform the pier into virtually any setting any film director could want, such as the 1930s for scenes from *The Glenn Miller Story* (1954) and *The Sting* (1973), a 1956 Los Angeles pier for the television movie *Private Eye* (1987) or to much more modern times as depicted in *The Big Trade* (1983) and in television's *Charlie's Angels, Marcus Welby, M.D., CHiPs, Simon & Simon* (1986) and *Hunter* (1987).

As a note of interest, the pier was also seen in the motion picture *Stranger Bargain*, a 1949 film that was reworked into a 1987 episode of television's *Murder, She Wrote*, featuring Martha Scott and Jeffrey Lynn, the actors who appeared in the 1949 film.

The pier, however, gained the most popularity due to the opening and closing scenes of television's *Three's Company* that were filmed in front of the famous "Sinbad's" and at the nearby electric bumper car ride at a small amusement center for the 1980 and 1981 television seasons.

The pier is located at the end of Colorado Avenue, west of Ocean Avenue in Santa Monica.

*Thomas Brothers Map reference: page 49 at A6. **1992 revised edition: page 671 at E3.***

This section of the Santa Monica Pier was a location for segments of *Inside Daisy Clover* (1965) and *The Glenn Miller Story* (1954) and in segments of television's *Three's Company* and other films and television series listed in this section. (Photos taken in 1986.)

Mission: Impossible (1966 to 1973)

The original version of this action series with an international intrigue flavor first aired on September 17, 1966, and concluded its lengthy run on September 8, 1973. Although not in the initial episodes of the series, Peter Graves in the role of James Phelps became the actor most associated with the I.M.F. team.

The I.M.F. (Impossible Mission Force) carried out a myriad of assignments throughout the world that were mostly filmed in the production company studios or in the greater Los Angeles area.

One location used several times in this series is the Fisherman's Village, a Marina del Rey landmark boasting Cape Cod-style buildings and adjoining boat docks that prove to be ideal for practically any scene dealing with the waterfront.

Other television series filmed here were *The Mod Squad*, *The F.B.I.* and *Trapper John*.

The village is located at 13723 Fiji Way in the Marina del Rey section of Los Angeles.

Thomas Brothers Map reference: page 49 at E6. 1992 revised edition: page 702 at B1.

Marina del Rey's Fisherman's Village and lighthouse, seen in television's *Mission: Impossible*, *The Mod Squad*, *The F.B.I.* and *Trapper John*. (Photos taken in 1986.)

────── The Silver Lake District ──────

Growing Pains (1985 to 1992)

This situation comedy was first telecast on September 24, 1985, and was immediately compared with *Father Knows Best,* a situation comedy that ran on television for nearly nine years from October 3, 1954, to April 5, 1963.

Comparison aside, *Growing Pains* is the saga of a New York psychiatrist, Dr. Jason Seaver (Alan Thicke), and his wife (Joanna Kerns) who do their best in today's world to raise their children.

As *Growing Pains* progressed through the television seasons, the young Seavers, Mike (Kirk Cameron), Carol (Tracey Gold), and Ben (Jeremy Miller) attended Thomas E. Dewey High School at various times, raising havoc with the school's staff. The school the Seavers actually attended in the series was John Marshall High School in Los Angeles.

John Marshall High School was also the location for a lengthy prom sequence seen in *Highway to Heaven,* a television drama created by the late actor/writer/producer Michael Landon, who regularly appeared as Jonathan, an angel on probation here on earth with the mission of bringing love and understanding into the lives of mortals in need. His constant companion in the series was an ex-cop named Mark (the late Victor French).

A favorite film location, Marshall High has been seen in many television series, including *L.A. Law* and *Uncle Buck.*

The building is located at 3101 Griffith Park Boulevard in the Los Feliz area of Los Angeles overlooking the site of the original Walt Disney Studios at 2719 Hyperion Avenue. The tower of the school can be seen in vintage photographs of the Walt Disney Studios.

The site of the high school building seen in most location shots is located on Tracy Street, west of St. George Street.

John Marshall High School and the site of the Walt Disney Studios are west of the Golden State Freeway (5).

Thomas Brothers Map reference: page 35 at A2. 1992 revised edition: page 594 at C3.

The tower and Tracy Street entrance to John Marshall High School in *Growing Pains,
Highway to Heaven, L.A. Law* and *Uncle Buck*. (Photos taken in 1990.)

Hi'-Neighbor! (1934)

The Hal Roach Studios camera crew ventured into Los Angeles from tiny Culver City in 1934 to film many scenes for this Our Gang comedy. The plot was typical Our Gang. The Gang's Wally (Wally Albright) tries to impress his girl (Jacqueline Taylor) by building a fire engine from junk to compete with a rich kid (Jerry Tucker) who just moved into the neighborhood with a small, custom-built fire engine, complete with a wood ladder.

Wally offers to race his fire engine against Jerry's to prove who has the fastest. As the race is about to begin from the top of a steep hill, Jerry smugly asks the Gang: "What's the matter, you afraid of a little hill?" Gang member "Stymie" (Matthew Beard) looks down the hill, swallows hard and replies, "What hill?"

The hill the Hal Roach Studios camera crew chose to film this scene is not the actual location used later for the lengthy fire engine race. That location had a much safer incline to assure protection for the studio crew and the members of Our Gang.

The camera crew ascended Fargo Street on Fargo Hill, the fifth steepest street in Los Angeles. It has a 32° grade. The hill and the street look much the same today as they did during the filming for this comedy.

The busy intersection at the base of Fargo Hill seen in the film is Glendale Boulevard and Fargo Street. (Glendale Boulevard at that point now leads directly into the Glendale Freeway.) The large building seen across Glendale Boulevard in the film is St. Teresa's Church. It was erected in 1929. The address is 2210 Fargo Street.

Fargo Hill (Fargo Street) is between Allesandro Street and Alvarado Street, east of the Glendale Freeway (2) and south of the Golden State Freeway (5) in Los Angeles.

Thomas Brothers Map reference: page 35 at C4. 1992 revised edition: page 594 at E5.

Fargo Street from the top of Fargo Hill, a very steep street (a 32 degree grade) seen at the beginning of the Our Gang race in *Hi'-Neighbor!* (Photo taken in 1986.)

St. Teresa's Church at the foot of Fargo Hill, seen in the same race segment of *Hi'-Neighbor!* (Photo taken in 1988.)

Max Monroe: Loose Cannon (1990)

Max Monroe (Shadoe Stevens) was the new kid on the block, so to speak, in television's police dramas. The program debuted on national television on January 5, 1990, and lasted for only a few episodes, ending in 1990. The plot centered on Monroe, a chess wizard who was also a Los Angeles police detective. He was teamed with a so-called logical partner by the name of Charlie (Bruce A. Young). The two got into and out of more complicated crime situations in one episode than most real-life detectives do in a career.

The city's Queen of Angels Hospital (now closed and used for motion picture/television series filming) is seen in the opening logo of the series. The building was also the primary location for the "Voices" episode of the series that aired on January 19, 1990, wherein Max and Charlie, aided by a blind physiotherapist, pursued and apprehended the killer of a doctor. And the building was a Wauchula, Florida, hospital in the 1991 mini-series *Switched at Birth*.

The Queen of Angeles Hospital facility is located on Bellevue Avenue, between Coronado Street and Waterloo Street, north of the Hollywood Freeway (101).

Thomas Brothers Map reference: page 35 at B6. 1992 revised edition: page 634 at D1.

The Queen of Angels Hospital, a film location seen in television's *Max Monroe: Loose Cannon* and in the 1991 television mini-series *Switched at Birth*. (Photos taken in 1989.)

The Music Box (1932)

Laurel and Hardy fans and buffs consider this the best short subject the duo made during their lengthy career. This fact is supported by the Academy of Motion Picture Arts and Sciences as the film won the Academy Award for the Best Live Action Comedy Short Subject for 1931/1932.

Now in the delivery business, Stan Laurel and Oliver Hardy contract to deliver a piano to 1127 Walnut Avenue. The instrument is a surprise gift for husband (Billy Gilbert) from his adoring wife (Gladys Gale).

When Laurel and Hardy arrive in the neighborhood with their horse-drawn wagon they quickly discover that the address they seek is a house high on top of a hill, at the end of a very long flight of stairs, pointed out to them by a passing postman (Charlie Hall).

Throughout a very long day, Laurel and Hardy struggle with the crated piano, attempting to get it to the top of the stairway.

The famous stairway scene was filmed between 923 and 925 Vendome Street in Los Angeles. The stairway has changed little over the decades but, much to the disappointment of the Laurel and Hardy faithful, now has a handrail and several light poles, installed by the City of Los Angeles for safety reasons.

In case anyone is curious, the number of steps that make up this famous stairway is 131.

The neighborhood, now in a rundown condition, has changed little structurally. In fact, a small stucco duplex seen in this film as Laurel and Hardy arrive with the piano still stands on a corner across Vendome Street from the foot of the stairway. Its dual address is 934 Vendome Street/3025 Del Monte Drive.

This film site was undoubtedly a Hal Roach Studios favorite as five years earlier, in 1927, door-to-door salesmen Laurel and Hardy struggled up and down the same stairway, this time with a clumsy washing machine, in their comedy classic *Hats Off*. As the two finally arrived at the top of the stairway, they met a prospective customer, lovely Anita Garvin, in front of a house at 3278 Descanso Drive. This house still stands today, virtually unchanged from the time of filming.

Disappointed at the lack of any sale, Laurel and Hardy travel on in *Hats Off*, ending up in the middle of Venice Boulevard and Bagley Avenue in Los Angeles, near Culver City, engaged in a wild fight with a group of men, the primary purpose being to destroy each other's hats.

As a note of interest, on April 21, 1982, the Los Angeles Cultural Heritage Board considered the stairway seen in these films as a cultural heritage location. The proposal was shelved, much to the disappointment of Laurel and Hardy fans worldwide, but will be reconsidered at a later date.

This film location is in danger of being demolished, however, as I learned that a freeway extension is being considered for the area and would run directly through this neighborhood, making the famous stairway but a memory.

The stairway location is north of the Hollywood Freeway (101). The "hat fight" location is south of the Santa Monica Freeway (10).

Thomas Brothers Map reference: page 35 at B5 (stairway). 1992 revised edition: page 594 at C6; page 42 at C6 (hat fight); 1992 revised edition: page 672 at G1.

The world famous stairway, the location of Laurel and Hardy's *The Music Box* (1932) and *Hats Off* (1927), located between 923 and 935 Vendome Street. (Photo taken in 1984.)

The top of the stairway, on Descanso Drive, and the house (3278) where Laurel and Hardy met Anita Garvin in *Hats Off.* (Photo taken in 1982.)

The duplex facing Del Monte Drive (3025) seen as Laurel and Hardy arrived to deliver the piano in the opening segment of *The Music Box.* (Photo taken in 1982.)

Venice Boulevard and Bagley Avenue where Laurel and Hardy and a group of men fought in the middle of the intersection during the final scene of *Hats Off*. (Photo taken in 1982.)

Rebel Without a Cause (1955)

Actor James Dean skyrocketed to stardom while becoming a symbol of the younger generation in this now classic film directed by Nicholas Ray.

A Los Angeles landmark, the Griffith Observatory in Griffith Park, has been a location for motion picture and television series production companies for over 50 years. Of the many scenes for the scores of motion pictures shot here, the scenes for this James Dean classic are by far the most popular with the man's countless fans.

One lengthy scene for the film was shot in front of the main observatory building with the Astronomers' Monument very evident. This classic 40-foot high stone monument is dedicated to astronomers Sir William Herschel, Sir Isaac Newton, Johannes Kepler, Nicolaus Copernicus, Galileo Galilei and Hipparchus. Figures of each astronomer surround the base of the monument that was a WPA (Works Progress Administration) project in the Great Depression years of the 1930s.

In this particular scene, Dean rested on a bench. But for those who might come to this location hoping to find the bench Dean sat on, be prepared for disappointment. It was removed many years ago. But a statue of Dean now stands near the bench site.

Sal Mineo (Dean's pal in the film) received an Academy Award nomination for Best Supporting Actor, Natalie Wood (Dean's girlfriend in the film) for Best Supporting Actress and Nicholas Ray for Writing (Motion Picture Story Category).

Other motion pictures filmed at this location are *The Dark City* (1950) and *The Terminator* (1984). Scenes for television's *Bionic Woman, Battlestar Galactica* and *The Colbys* were also filmed at this location.

Movie serial fans and the fans of Gene Autry will be pleased to learn that the observatory building was a part of the underground kingdom of Murania which was located 20,000 feet below the surface of Autry's Radio Ranch in the Mascot serial *The Phantom Empire* (1935).

The Griffith Observatory is #168 in the city's Historical Cultural Monument listing.

The observatory is located in Griffith Park at 2800 E. Observatory Road, north of Los Feliz Boulevard and west of the Golden State Freeway (5).

*Thomas Brothers Map reference: page 34 at E1. **1992 revised edition: page 593 at J2.***

Top: The Griffith Observatory, a location seen in *Rebel Without a Cause* (1955), *The Dark City* (1950) and *The Terminator* (1984) as well as in the television series listed in this section. (Photo taken in 1986.) *Bottom:* The Astronomer's Monument at the observatory seen in *Rebel Without a Cause* and *The Terminator*. (Photo taken in 1986.)

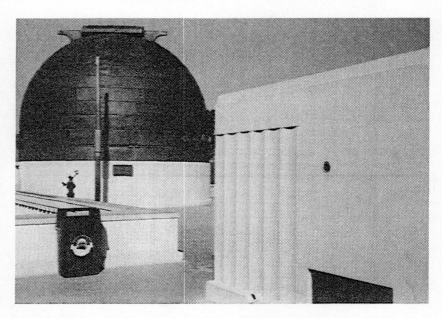

The observatory's dome and wall seen in *The Phantom Empire* as part of Murania. (Photo taken in 1986.)

The observatory's west stairway that led to the entrance of a building in Murania in *The Phantom Empire*. (Photo taken in 1986.)

—————————— Simi Valley ——————————

The Adventures of Robin Hood (1938)

The huge oak forest on the old Corrigan Ranch (now known as Hopeville) in the small community of Simi Valley, served as the Sherwood Forest for several scenes of this Errol Flynn motion picture classic wherein Flynn won the hand of Maid Marian (Olivia de Havilland) while fighting the ruthless Prince John (Claude Rains) and the evil Sir Guy of Gisbourne (Basil Rathbone).

Within this forest is a large man-made cement basin, now dry, that served the motion picture industry as a lake when necessary. A waterproof camera room, used to film underwater scenes, is located at the west end of the basin. A rock bluff, also man-made, situated on the north side of the basin, once served as a location for countless fight scenes where the bad guys and the good guys as well were knocked from it or fell from it into the water as did many horses, buckboards and a stagecoach or two at the hectic conclusion of exciting chase scenes.

This bluff, the lake and the nearby oak trees were prominent in a scene from the motion picture *Impact,* a 1949 film that starred Brian Donlevy and Ella Raines.

Literally hundreds of Hollywood features were filmed at this location, mostly Westerns by Monogram, Republic and PRC Studios which include Roy Rogers' *Cowboy and the Senorita* (1944), *Along the Navajo Trail* (1945), *Susanna Pass* (1946), *Down Dakota Way* (1949) and *Twilight in the Sierras* (1950); Gene Autry's *The Hills of Utah* (1951) and Ken Maynard's *Harmony Trail* (1944).

The Adventures of Robin Hood won three Academy Awards; Eric Wolfgang Korngold for his Outstanding Musical Score; Carl J. Weyl for Interior Decoration and Ralph Dawson for Editing.

The ranch is located on Kuehner Drive at Smith Road, south of the Simi Valley Freeway (118) in Simi Valley. The Sherwood Forest is at the east end of the ranch. It can be reached by driving east on Smith Road to its end, then east on a dirt road to the ranch gate. Once past the gate, continue east to the forest and the lake.

Thomas Brothers Map reference: Ventura County edition: page 67 at F2. 1992 revised Los Angeles County edition: page 499 at C3.

Top: The Corrigan Ranch oak forest, a location for some scenes of *The Adventures of Robin Hood* (1938), *Impact* (1949) and the Western films listed in this section. (Photo taken in 1986.) *Bottom:* The lakebed and the artificial cliff (left side of photo) seen in *Impact* and the Western films listed in this section. (Photo taken in 1986.)

The room at the end of the lakebed (center of photo) was used to house camera equipment for underwater shots. (Photo taken in 1986.)

A buckboard and an old car were but two of many vehicles that flipped and crashed here at the conclusion of many exciting chase scenes. (Photo taken in 1986.)

Here Come the Co-Eds (1945)

I've been contacted many times over the years by Bud Abbott and Lou Costello fans who request film locations of that famous comedy team. This is a difficult task as the majority of the scenes from their many films were shot on the Universal Studios lot. I did, however, come up with one. It's the train/trailer chase location seen near the conclusion of this film.

A girls' school is the primary setting for the film. Abbott and Costello portray caretakers who fumble their way into solving the institution's financial crisis despite the villainy of Lon Chaney, Jr.

The scene begins as Lou steals money from gamblers. He is joined in an escape attempt by Bud. The two quickly hitch a ride on a small sailboat being towed by a station wagon. The boat soon breaks loose from the station wagon and Bud and Lou hoist the sail to take advantage of the wind in order to keep ahead of pursuing Chaney and his pal in crime. They go on a crazy ride through Los Angeles streets, finally ending up on a single stretch of railroad tracks where an approaching passenger train passes them in a dark tunnel.

This scene took place in part in the Santa Susana Pass Wash, a location where railroad tracks follow Santa Susana Pass Road and go under Topanga Canyon Boulevard via a tunnel.

This location is very close to the Iverson Movie Ranch and I suggest you include a stop there while visiting the ranch.

The railroad tracks and the tunnel are south of the Simi Valley Freeway (118) and west of Topanga Canyon Boulevard (27).

Exit the Simi Valley Freeway at Topanga Canyon Boulevard. Go south a short distance (the first intersection) to Santa Susana Pass Road. Turn right. Go north on Santa Susana Pass Road approximately 100 yards. Park there. Cross Santa Sustana Pass Road to the railroad tracks. The tunnel will be on the right.

*Thomas Brothers Map reference: page 6 at C1. **1992 revised edition: page 500 at A2.***

The curved section of railroad track and the dark tunnel where Abbott and Costello encounter a speeding train in the closing segment of *Here Come the Co-Eds.* (Photos taken in 1986.)

────── West Los Angeles ──────

Block-Heads (1938)

This motion picture was planned to be the last in the lengthy film career of comic legends Stan Laurel and Oliver Hardy. It wasn't. Twelve additional features followed. Sadly, however, this proved to be the last outstanding comedy the duo made.

The plot was simple for Laurel and Hardy and their fans. Hardy learns that Laurel now resides on the nearby Old Soldier's Home some 20 years after they were separated in battle in France during World War I. In rapid succession, Hardy goes to the Old Soldier's Home and brings Laurel home for dinner, much to the displeasure of Mrs. Hardy (Minna Gombell), who leaves in disgust, causing the two to cook for themselves.

The end result is a gas stove explosion that virtually destroys the Hardy kitchen. A neighbor (Patricia Ellis) offers to help clean up the mess but her jealous husband (Billy Gilbert) doesn't understand, finally chasing Laurel and Hardy from the apartment building, firing his shotgun wildly into the air.

This closing scene, used 10 years earlier (1928) in their short comedy *We Faw Down*, shows the two running for their lives between two large apartment buildings as scores of trouserless men jump from the apartment windows.

The scene near the opening of the film where Hardy finds Laurel at the Old Soldiers Home was shot on the grounds of the Veterans Administration complex in West Los Angeles. The Old Soldiers Home seen in the film was demolished years ago to make way for more modern facilities. The entrance to the complex, seen in the film, is as it was in 1938. A Veterans Administration plaque affixed to a pillar at this location was seen in the film. In fact, this plaque is all that remains today to identify this location as a certified Laurel and Hardy film location.

The apartment buildings seen at the close of the film, however, remain intact and look the same today. The exact location of the filming can be observed from the sidewalk on 8th Street, between the buildings, looking south.

The entrance (film site) to the Veterans Administration complex is at the intersection of Sawtelle Boulevard and Ohio Street, west of the San Diego Freeway (405). The apartment buildings are the St. Arthur Apartments, 2014 W. 8th Street and the Westmont, 807 S. Westlake Avenue, east of Alvarado Street, south of Wilshire Boulevard and north of the Santa Monica Freeway (10) near downtown Los Angeles.

Thomas Brothers Map reference: page 41 at D3 (Veteran Administration.). 1992 revised edition: page 632 at A5; page 44 at B2 (apartment buildings); 1992 revised edition: page 634 at C3.

The plaque and pillar at the Sawtelle Boulevard entrance to the Veterans Administration grounds seen in *Block-Heads*. (Photo taken in 1982.)

The location in the center of the Veterans Administration grounds where Hardy pushed Laurel toward Hardy's car in a wheelchair. (Photo taken in 1990.)

The two apartment buildings seen in *Block-Heads,* viewed from 8th Street. (Photo taken in 1987.)

A close-up of the location between the two apartment buildings seen in the closing segment of *Block-Heads.* (Photo taken in 1987.)

Bouncing Babies (1929)

In this early Our Gang film, Wheezer's (Bobby Hutchins) mother has a baby, making it the center of family attention in place of Wheezer. Understandably, the boy becomes jealous, so much so that he plans to return the baby to the hospital which is located on the opposite side of a very busy boulevard.

Pushing the baby in a large crib with wheels, Wheezer approaches the boulevard. As no traffic controls are present, he looks about and finds a box of large light bulbs in front of a store near the corner. He quickly tosses one into the street. The loud pop causes all traffic to stop, the concerned drivers jumping from their vehicles to check their tires. So successful is this scheme that Wheezer uses it several times to cross the busy street until two motorcycle policemen intervene.

The busy boulevard seen in this film was Motor Avenue and the cross street was Tabor Street. The large building on the corner where Wheezer found the box of light bulbs housed Bacon's Pharmacy and Safeway Stores, Inc., during filming. The building is now occupied by a cleaner/laundromat and a market under a different name. Surprisingly, it is virtually unchanged since filming in 1929. The address is 3568/3570 Motor Avenue, Los Angeles.

This location is south of the Santa Monica Freeway (10).

*Thomas Brothers Map reference: page 42 at B6. **1992 revised edition: page 672 at F1.***

A building on Motor Avenue, a primary film location in *Bouncing Babies* as "Wheezer" attempts to cross a busy street. (Photo taken in 1988.)

Boxing Gloves (1929)

This Our Gang film was released on September 9, 1929, and billed as an "all-talking" feature when, in fact, it contained many scenes that were entirely silent.

The plot centered on the big fight between the two very heavy members of the Gang, Chubby (Norman Chaney) and Joe Cobb. The only problem was that the two were friends and didn't want to fight. Both boys, however, were fond of beautiful Jean Darling who played Chubby against Joe and Joe against Chubby in typical kid fashion.

In one scene, Joe and Chubby, at Jean's request, run back and forth from Jean to a nearby food wagon to bring Jean a bottle of her favorite soft drink. As the two "heavies" pass each other, they expectedly bump into each other until one finally drops Jean's bottle of pop onto the sidewalk, smashing it to bits.

This action takes place in front of a brick building located on the corner of Motor Avenue and Woodbine Street in Los Angeles, only two blocks west of the *Bouncing Babies* film location.

The film location is south of the Santa Monica Freeway (10).

Thomas Brothers Map reference: page 42 at B5. 1992 revised edition: page 632 at F7.

A corner building on Motor Avenue, a primary film location in *Boxing Gloves* where "Chubby" and Joe ran past each other several times to get a soda for Jean Darling. (Photo taken in 1985.)

Chinatown (1974)

In this 1930s suspense motion picture, Jack Nicholson portrays a Los Angeles private detective who becomes deeply involved in murder and political corruption directly related to a fortune in land and water rights in the city's vast San Fernando Valley.

The beautiful Spanish-style building seen in the latter part of this film as the "Mar Vista Rest Home" is the Eastern Star Home located in the Brentwood section of Los Angeles.

Nicholson and co-star Faye Dunaway drive to the rest home through the Valley to conduct an investigation. This action is prompted by an article in a newspaper clipping that relates to a memorial service held there. The building is referred to as the "Mar Vista Inn" in the clipping. I assume this is a production company error.

Nicholson and Dunaway enter the building, talk to the manager about placing Nicholson's father in the home (a ruse to check the building out), then inspect the building's facilities. Their snooping leads to a rather brutal confrontation between Nicholson and some rough-looking men. As Dunaway drives Nicholson away, several shots are fired at their vehicle.

As water use was an integral part of the film's plot, director Roman Polanski chose the Hollywood Reservoir as a background for several scenes. Situated deep in the Hollywood Hills above the film capital, the reservoir has served as a film location over the decades. Dedicated in 1925, it is a part of a vast network of waterways that provides the city of Los Angeles with precious water. In fact, this single body of water serves more than 400,000 persons daily.

Scenes for the motion picture *Out of Bounds* were filmed here in 1986, and the reservoir waters threatened to inundate the city below in the disaster epic *Earthquake* in 1974.

The Eastern Star Home, also seen as a hospital in a 1988 *Hunter* episode, is located at 11725 Sunset Boulevard, west of the San Diego Freeway (405) and north of Wilshire Boulevard.

The Hollywood Reservoir is located east of the Hollywood Freeway (101) and east of Barham Boulevard at the terminus of Lake Hollywood Drive in Hollywood. Another approach is from the opposite side of the reservoir, north of the Hollywood Freeway (101) and Franklin Avenue and east of Cahuenga Boulevard, at the end of Weidlake Drive in Hollywood.

Thomas Brothers Map reference: page 41 at C1 (Eastern Star Home). 1992 revised edition: page 631 at H2; page 24 at C6 (Lake Hollywood Drive); 1992 revised edition: page 593 at E1; page 34 at C1 (Weidlake Drive); 1992 revised edition: page 593 at F2.

The west end (top photo) and the east end (bottom photo) of the Eastern Star Home
seen in television's *Hunter* and in *Chinatown* as Jack Nicholson and Faye Dunaway
slowly approach then rapidly depart. (Photos taken in 1989.)

The Hollywood Reservoir that threatened the city of Los Angeles, seen in *Earthquake* (1974). (Photo taken in 1987.)

The shoreline of the reservoir seen in *Chinatown* (1974) and in *Out of Bounds* (1986). (Photo taken in 1987.)

The Finishing Touch (1928)

Carpenters Stan Laurel and Oliver Hardy are hired by the owner of a half-finished house (Sam Lufkin) to complete the work by noon the following day. A problem soon arises as the building site is near a hospital where unnecessary noise can't be tolerated. Laurel and Hardy try to be as quiet as possible but fail. A nurse (Dorothy Coburn) from the hospital complains to a cop (Edgar Kennedy) who vows to make sure the peace of the neighborhood is kept, especially by Laurel and Hardy.

The two carpenters somehow complete the job and are paid in full. But the house quickly begins to fall apart and Lufkin demands a refund.

The film site is just north of Club Drive at 2818/2826 Motor Avenue in Cheviot Hills. Two houses now occupy the site that was a vacant lot during filming, the house seen in the film being nothing but studio props.

A house located across the street from the film site, at 2817 Motor Avenue, was seen throughout the film and looks the same today as it did in 1928.

This location is north of the Santa Monica Freeway (10).

*Thomas Brothers Map reference: page 42 at B4. **1992 revised edition:** page 632 at F6.*

A Spanish-style two-story house on the east side of Motor Avenue now occupies the site of the prop house seen in *The Finishing Touch*.

Across Motor Avenue, at 2817, is a Spanish-style house seen in *The Finishing Touch*. (Photo taken in 1987.)

Fly My Kite (1931)

For an Our Gang comedy, this entry has a rather sad plot.

An old lady the Gang calls "Grandma" (Margaret Mann) is about to be kicked out of her house and put in an "old folks' home" by her son-in-law (James Mason) who hates her. Grandma, although broke, does have a stack of old gold bonds she thinks have no value. A letter arrives at Grandma's house and is intercepted by Mason who learns that the bonds have a value of $100,000.

Before Mason can confront Grandma, she gives the bonds to the Gang to add weight to the tail of a kite they are attempting to fly in a field across the street from her house. Mason learns where the bonds are and hurries to the field to snatch them from the Gang's kite. Then the fun begins.

Grandma's old wood house, demolished years ago, was located on Overland Avenue and Venice Boulevard in Los Angeles, near Culver City. Three houses near Grandma's house that were seen in the film in 1931, although rapidly showing their age, still stand on the east side of Overland Avenue. The addresses are 3650, 3658 and 3668.

The field where the kite flying scene was filmed is located across the street from the three houses. It is now occupied by several apartment buildings.

This location is south of the Santa Monica Freeway (10).

Thomas Brothers Map reference: page 42 at B6. 1992 revised edition: page 672 at F1.

The following three houses were seen in *Fly My Kite*, located across the street from "Grandma's" house.

3650 Overland Avenue. (Photo taken in 1984.)

3658 Overland Avenue. (Photo taken in 1988.)

3668 Overland Avenue. (Photo taken in 1988.)

The site of the field on the opposite (west) side of Motor Avenue where the kite flying segment of *Fly My Kite* was shot, now occupied by an apartment building. (Photo taken in 1984.)

Honkey Donkey (1934)

One day shy of three months from the release date of Our Gang's *Hi'-Neighbor!* (March 3, 1934/June 2, 1934), the Gang's Wally (Wally Albright) is now cast as a rich kid whose overprotective mother instructs her chauffeur (Don Barclay) to "Take very good care of Wallace all the way home" after she exits the family limousine to begin a shopping spree in downtown Culver City.

Wally, however, has other ideas and instructs Barclay to turn the limousine around and to "Drive through some alleys—some dirty ones."

The trip is short as the alley Barclay finds is just across the street from Culver City in Los Angeles. The alley is north of Venice Boulevard, between Bagley Avenue and Cardiff Street, providing service access to the businesses that line Venice Boulevard much as it did in 1934.

Once in the alley, Barclay rolls to a stop near the Gang who are playing with a mule in front of an old barn that was up for sale. This location was at the nearby Hal Roach Studios and the scene was shot in its entirety there.

The alley film location is south of the Santa Monica Freeway (10) in the Palms section of Los Angeles.

*Thomas Brothers Map reference: page 42 at C6. **1992 revised edition:** page 672 at G1.*

Top: The alley seen in *Honkey Donkey,* looking west from Bagley Avenue toward Cardiff Avenue. (Photo taken in 1986.) *Bottom:* Bagley Avenue, looking south toward downtown Culver City was another location seen in the film. The alley is behind the building on the right. The building seen in *Hats Off* and *Bacon Grabbers* is on the left. (Photo taken in 1985.)

Hook and Ladder (1932)

Most kids in the 1930s and 1940s seemed to want to grow up to be firemen, and the members of Our Gang were no exception in this 1932 film.

As the film opens, the Gang responds to a public appeal to assist local fire departments by founding a fire department of their own. The first step is to convert an old barn into a fire station and create a fire engine to be pulled by a horse. The chief's car is made out of scrap wood.

A column of smoke soon arises on the horizon and the Gang is off through Los Angeles streets near the Culver City city limits to, of all places, the local fire station which is empty as the real fire engines have responded to the "real" fire.

The wide street the Gang's fire apparatus raced down toward the fire station was Motor Avenue, between Woodbine Street and National Boulevard.

The fire station seen in the film as the Gang arrived was actually the neighborhood fire station. It was the home of Los Angeles City Engine Co. 43 which has now relocated several blocks away.

The old fire station building stands today, now converted to house a series of small shops. The address is 10420 National Boulevard, Los Angeles.

This location is south of the Santa Monica Freeway (10).

Thomas Brothers Map reference: page 42 at B5. 1992 revised edition: page 632 at E7.

Top: The building that housed the old Engine Co. 43 on National Boulevard, a primary film location in *Hook and Ladder* as Our Gang members responded to their first fire alarm. (Photo taken in 1988.) *Bottom:* Motor Avenue, between Woodbine Street and National Boulevard, the street location where Our Gang's fire apparatus raced toward a fire in *Hook and Ladder*. (Photo taken in 1984.)

Lazy Days (1929)

Hal Roach Studios utilized the surrounding Culver City neighborhoods regularly to film various segments of their comedies, especially the downtown area. This Our Gang short is no exception. In fact, the majority of the scenes in this film were shot in a small park, fittingly named Media Park, located but a few blocks from the studios.

The plot revolves around the Gang who are interested in entering a baby contest for the $50 first prize.

"Farina" (Allen Hoskins) is featured with Pete the Pup and the rest of the Gang.

Media Park is a short distance down the street (north) from the intersection of Venice Boulevard and Bagley Avenue, a film location seen in the Laurel and Hardy comedies *Hats Off* (1927) and *Bacon Grabbers* (1929) and Our Gang's *Honkey Donkey* (1934).

The park is triangular and is bounded by Canfield Avenue, Venice Boulevard and Washington Boulevard, in Los Angeles just outside the Culver City city limits.

*Thomas Brothers Map reference: page 42 at C6. **1992 revised edition:** page 632 at H7.*

Media Park, a primary film location seen in *Lazy Days* where Our Gang's "Farina" relaxed. (Photo taken in 1988.)

The northeast corner of Media Park, looking west on Venice Boulevard toward Bagley Avenue. (Photo taken in 1988.)

Perfect Day (1929)

The plot of this film is typical Laurel and Hardy. The two, their wives (Kay Deslys and Isabelle Keith) and Uncle Edgar (Edgar Kennedy) who is suffering with the gout, plan a Sunday picnic instead of attending church. As all prepare to leave, a food fight erupts, with a large tray of sandwiches providing the weapons. This minor dispute finally settled, the quintet leave the house only to fall into a series of interruptions, the most serious being their parson (Charley Rogers) strolling by en route to church.

Successfully ducking Rogers, Laurel and Hardy endure a flat tire on their Model "T" and a heated argument with a neighbor (Baldwin Cooke) who throws their car jack through the vehicle's windshield in retaliation for Hardy tossing the jack at Cooke's home in anger. All of this is viewed by neighbors (Harry Bernard and Clara Guiol) who show only a mild interest.

The majority of the exterior scenes for this film were shot on a narrow side street west of Venice Boulevard in Los Angeles that remains unchanged today.

The "Perfect Day" house is located at 3120 Vera Avenue. The address of the house next door where Hardy tossed the car jack through the window is 3116 Vera Avenue. The address of the neighbor's house across the street is 3115 Vera Avenue.

All houses are located south of the Santa Monica Freeway (10).

Thomas Brothers Map reference: page 42 at D5. 1992 revised edition: page 632 at H7.

Laurel and Hardy's home on Vera Avenue (3120) seen throughout *Perfect Day*. (Photo taken in 1982.)

The house next door to Laurel and Hardy's house in *Perfect Day*, the location of the "fight" scene. The address is 3116 Vera Avenue. (Photo taken in 1988.)

The house across the street (3115 Vera Avenue) seen in *Perfect Day* where friendly neighbors called out many good-byes during the final scenes of the film. (Photo taken in 1982.)

Pigskin Palooka (1937)

While attending a military academy in a distant city, Our Gang's Alfalfa (Carl Switzer) writes home to his girl (Darla Hood) in Culver City, bragging about his football exploits for the academy team. Actually, Alfalfa doesn't know one end of a football from the other.

When he arrives home on a train Alfalfa meets reality in a big way when he is immediately recruited for the big game between Spanky's (George McFarland) football all-stars and a rival team consisting of the toughest kids in the neighborhood headed by Our Gang actor Dickie Jones.

Alfalfa's train arrival was filmed at the Palms Railroad Station in the Palms section of Los Angeles, near Culver City. The Hal Roach Studios also used this station and the immediate vicinity to film segments of Laurel and Hardy's *Berth Marks* in 1929.

This ornate railroad station was typical of the early railroad stations that dotted the Los Angeles landscape and is one of the few remaining wood structures that date back to the steam railroads. Thankfully, the station was rescued intact and relocated before the wrecker's ball reached it.

The Palms Railroad Station has been restored and is now permanently located in Heritage Square, a historical park dedicated to the re-creation of Victorian Los Angeles of the period from 1885 to 1915.

As related in the *Choo-Choo!* section of this book, Stan Laurel and Oliver Hardy began their trip to Pottsville in 1929 at the old Santa Fe Railroad Station in downtown Los Angeles.

Eager to earn a few dollars, the two "musicians" buy their tickets at the station, then almost miss the slowly departing train when they drop a bundle of sheet music.

Safely on the train, Laurel and Hardy decide to retire in order to be rested for their Pottsville performance. A single berth is just too small for the two and changing from their street clothing into nightshirts proves to be nearly impossible.

When the two are finally settled, the train's conductor (Silas D. Wilcox) loudly announces: "Next stop is Pottsville! All out for Pottsville!"

Now in a panic, Laurel and Hardy scramble to gather their clothing and get off the train. They accomplish this task, their hats on their heads, their clothing in their hands, standing on the station platform in their underwear. Hardy then learns that Laurel forgot their musical instrument which was left on the train now disappearing around a curve of the tracks. Infuriated, Hardy chases Laurel down the tracks, throwing a rock at him as the film ends.

As a note of interest, the Palms station location signs now on the building were painted by railroad enthusiast Ward Kimball, formerly an animator with the Walt Disney Studios and a musician in the famed Firehouse Five Plus Two Dixieland Band.

The site of the Palms Railroad Station where everyone got off the train is situated behind a furniture manufacturing company that faces National Boulevard, next to the very busy Santa Monica Freeway, between Motor Avenue and Vinton Avenue in Los Angeles.

This film location is not easy to reach and one must be a rabid Our Gang and/or Laurel and Hardy fan to make the trek. I find it easiest to approach from near the intersection of National Boulevard and Motor Avenue by following the railroad tracks to the station's cement foundation. Another approach is from the opposite direction. To do this, begin near the intersection of Clarington Avenue and National Boulevard.

The Palms Railroad Station (Depot) is #22 in the city's Historical Cultural Monument listing.

Heritage Square is located at 3800 N. Homer Street, east of the Pasadena Freeway (110) in Los Angeles.

Thomas Brothers Map reference: page 42 at B5 (Palms Railroad Station site). 1992 revised edition: page 632 at F7; page 36 at B4 (Heritage Square); 1992 revised edition: page 595 at A6.

Top: The Palms Railroad Station, the film location of Our Gang's *Pigskin Palooka* (1937) and Laurel and Hardy's *Berth Marks* (1929), at its "new" and permanent location at Heritage Square. (Photo taken in 1988.) *Bottom:* The original foundation (1886/1976) of the Palms Railroad Station (next to the palm tree and behind the fence), near National Boulevard and Vinton Avenue. (Photo taken in 1988.)

Top: A cement section between the tracks is all that remains of the location where Laurel and Hardy and "Alfalfa" debarked from their respective trains in *Berth Marks* (1929) and *Pigskin Palooka* (1937). (Photo taken in 1986.) *Bottom:* The film location west of the site of the Palms Railroad Station where Hardy chased Laurel in the closing scene of *Berth Marks*. (Photo taken in 1988.)

Whittier

Back to the Future (1985)

This sci-fi comedy featured actor Michael J. Fox as a teenager who was transported back to the 1950s via a time machine automobile that was constructed by a rather strange inventor (Christopher Lloyd). Back in the 1950s, Fox meets his parents who, at that time, were his age.

The 1950s high school seen in this film was Whittier High School, an excellent choice by the film production company as today in the 1990s the entire school complex does indeed resemble a 1950s school.

The campus is located at 12417 Philadelphia Street, east of the San Gabriel River Freeway (605) and north of Whittier Boulevard.

Note: The sequel to this film, *Back to the Future II,* was filmed, in part, in North Hollywood. Please refer to the *Back to the Future II* section of this book for further information on that film location.

*Thomas Brothers Map reference: page 55 at D5. **1992 revised edition: page 677 at C6.***

The Whittier High School campus and buildings seen in *Back to the Future*. (Photos taken in 1989.)

—————— The Wilshire District ——————

The Adventures of Superman (1952 to 1957)

This adventure series featuring the Man of Steel began 30-minute television episodes in July of 1951 but did not actually appear on commercial television until late in 1952. The series continued until 1957. In all, a total of 104 episodes were broadcast.

The plot is well-known Americana, beginning in a comic book in 1938 and continuing in a newspaper strip for 28 years from 1939 to 1967. A radio series ran from 1940 to 1951, and 17 animated cartoons appeared in movie houses from 1941 to 1943 as did theatrical serials from 1948 to 1950. A full-length motion picture, *Superman and the Mole Men,* was released in 1951. This black and white feature was the forerunner of the color series that starred Christopher Reeve as the Man of Steel, beginning in 1978 with the 143 minute epic *Superman.* Three sequels followed.

Actor Kirk Alyn portrayed Clark Kent/Superman in the serials and in *Superman and the Mole Men.* Actor George Reeves of *Gone with the Wind* fame was the Man of Steel for the length of the television series.

Superman buffs and most Los Angeles residents are aware that the Los Angeles City Hall (minus its peaked top) was the Daily Planet Building in the television series, but few persons are aware that the lobby of the Carnation Building several miles west of downtown Los Angeles was the location used as the lobby of *The Daily Planet.* This was necessary as the lobby of the Los Angeles City Hall was simply too busy on a daily basis to accommodate a television production company's cast, crew and equipment that would be continually present to produce a weekly television program.

The Los Angeles City Hall, however, remains the most popular of the two buildings as it is as familiar to motion picture and television series fans as the world famous Hollywood sign atop nearby Mount Lee overlooking the film capital of the world. The byzantine interior of the building dates to a time of elegance. Completed in 1928, it is regularly seen today in scores of motion pictures and television series as the interior of the Senate Building in Washington, D.C., or the interior of a court building anywhere in the United States.

This interior was seen in *Mildred Pierce* (1945), *The Sunshine Boys* (1975), *Going Berserk* (1983), *Protocol* (1984), *Badge of the Assassin* (1985), *L.B.J.: The Early Years* (1987) and *Stillwatch* (1987) to name but a few. The famous "arched" west entrance was seen in *Dragnet* (1987), but found motion picture fame as the location of the opening scenes of *D.O.A.,* a film classic released in 1949 that starred Edmond O'Brien as a man slowly dying of poison, searching Los Angeles for his killer.

Other than the *Superman* series, many scenes for television's *Cagney & Lacey, Hill Street Blues, Highway to Heaven, The Colbys, Matlock, Twilight Zone* (1986), *L.A. Law, Murder, She Wrote, Jake and the Fatman* and *Dragnet* were filmed here.

As a note of interest, General George S. Patton reviewed World War II troops from the top of the west entrance stairway during the waining days of World War II.

The "Hollywood" sign atop Mount Lee is #111 in the city's Historical Cultural Monument listing.

The Los Angeles City Hall is #150 in the city's Historical Cultural Monument listing.

The Los Angeles City Hall is located at 200 N. Spring Street, south of the Hollywood Freeway (101) and east of the Harbor Freeway (110) in downtown Los Angeles.

The Carnation Building is located at 5045 Wilshire Boulevard in the Wilshire District of Los Angeles, north of the Santa Monica Freeway (10).

Thomas Brothers Map reference: page 44 at D3 (Los Angeles City Hall). 1992 revised edition: page 634 at G3; page 43 at B2 (Carnation Building); 1992 revised edition: page 633 at E2.

The Los Angeles City Hall, the exterior of the Daily Planet Building seen throughout *The Adventures of Superman* television series. (Photo taken in 1986.)

Top: The west entrance to the city hall where Gen. George S. Patton reviewed World War II troops. It was also a location seen in the *Dragnet* television series and in the motion picture *Dragnet* (1987). (Photo taken in 1986.) *Bottom:* The central hallway of the city hall, a location for segments of the motion picture *Mildred Pierce* (1945) and other motion pictures and television series listed in this section. (Photo taken in 1986.)

Top: The city hall garage exit on Main Street, north of 1st Street, a location regularly seen in the early episodes of television's *Dragnet.* (Photo taken in 1987.) *Bottom:* Wearing Los Angeles City Badge #1, George Mogelberg stands at his post (the Main Street entrance to the Los Angeles City Hall) where he was seen in many episodes of television's *Dragnet* and in the *Dragnet* (1954) motion picture. (Photo taken in the 1950s.)

Top: The Wilshire Boulevard entrance to the Carnation Building, the location of the lobby of *The Daily Planet* seen in *The Adventures of Superman* television series. (Photo taken in 1990.) *Bottom:* Another view of the Carnation Building from Wilshire Boulevard. (Photo taken in 1990.)

If I Had a Million (1932)

Comedian W.C. Fields was at his best in this series of short stories that revolve around a generous millionaire John Glidden (Richard Bennett) who suddenly decides to give his fortune away to strangers rather than to his greedy relatives. The names of the lucky strangers are taken from the pages of a local telephone directory.

Film historians agree that the segment of this film starring Fields and his buxom wife (Alison Skipworth) wherein the two purchase a new Ford, only to have the car demolished as they leave the new car dealership, is comedy at its best and may never be duplicated.

This film location was very hard to locate as the Ford agency long ago departed and the building was demolished. Buildings across the street from the agency as seen in the film remain the same today as they appeared in the film and were the key to authenticating this important site.

The site of the Ford agency (Jack Frost Ford — an actual Ford dealership in Los Angeles for decades) was at 750 S. La Brea Avenue. The location of the "crash" scene was on 8th Street, the south side of the building.

The film location is south of Wilshire Boulevard and north of the Santa Monica Freeway (10) in the Park La Brea section of Los Angeles.

Thomas Brothers Map reference: page 43 at B2. 1992 revised edition: page 633 at D3.

The site of the new car dealership seen in *If I Had a Million*. (Photo taken in 1986.)

The location of the famous W.C. Fields "crash" scene in *If I Had a Million*, on 8th Street, east of La Brea Avenue. (Photo taken in 1986.)

Typical California 1930s-style buildings on the south side of 8th Street, east of La Brea Avenue, seen in *If I Had a Million*. (Photo taken in 1986.)

The garage across 8th Street from the W.C. Fields "crash" site. (Photo taken in 1986.)

La Bamba (1987)

The classic Wiltern Theater, located in the Wilshire District of Los Angeles, was transformed into the Paramount/Brooklyn Theater in New York for the segment of this film wherein Ritchie Valens (Lou Diamond Phillips) gets his first big break in the music industry.

As 17-year-old Valens began to skyrocket to fame, he was summoned to New York to appear in Alan Freed's "Rock 'n' Roll" show. Valens followed the great Jackie Wilson's act and the rest is history.

Valens, sadly, died at age 17 in a 1959 plane crash that also took the lives of fellow musicians Buddy Holly and J.B. Richardson who was also known as "The Big Bopper." The Valens funeral procession seen near the end of this film traveled west on San Fernando Mission Boulevard, turned north onto Strandwood Avenue, then entered the Mission Cemetery, the actual location where Ritchie Valens rests.

It must be noted that the very popular musical group Los Lobos authentically recreated the 1950s music of Valens for this film.

Scenes from *American Hot Wax*, the 1978 film that depicted the rise and fall of Alan Freed, the popular disc jockey who gave Valens his New York break, were also filmed at the Wiltern as were scenes from *Beverly Hills Cop II*, the Eddie Murphy sequel to his *Beverly Hills Cop* blockbuster, and *Streets of Fire*, the 1984 rock 'n' roll fable that centered on a female rock star who was kidnapped by crazy bikers.

The San Fernando Mission was also the location of the classic Christmastime "Lost Baby Jesus" episode of Jack Webb's *Dragnet* in 1969.

The Wiltern Theater is located at 3790 Wilshire Boulevard, north of the Santa Monica Freeway (10).

The San Fernando Mission and the Mission Cemetery are located 11160 Strandwood Avenue, north of San Fernando Mission Boulevard, west of the Golden State Freeway (5) and east of the San Diego Freeway (405) in Mission Hills.

Thomas Brothers Map reference: page 43 at E2 (Wiltern Theater). 1992 revised edition: page 633 at H2; page 8 at C1 (San Francisco Mission and Cemetery); 1992 revised edition: page 501 at H2.

The Wiltern Theater, a film location for *La Bamba* (1987), *American Hot Wax* (1978), *Beverly Hills Cop II* (1987) and *Streets of Fire* (1984). (Photo taken in 1989.)

The San Fernando Mission Cemetery, the final resting place of the legendary Ritchie Valens. (Photo taken in 1986.)

Leave It to Beaver (1957 to 1963)

This classic situation comedy was first telecast on October 4, 1957, and lasted until September 12, 1963. All family events were vividly seen through the eyes of 7-year-old Beaver Cleaver (Jerry Mathers), and his 12-year-old brother Wally (Tony Dow). The little boy cuteness, however, wore thin as the seasons rolled by. Beaver got older and Wally was ready for college when the series finally ended.

As with many television programs (and motion pictures, for that matter) that somehow become classics, popular interest led to a revival. Beaver fans demanded more adventures of the Cleaver clan. Thus *The New Leave It to Beaver* television series became a reality and, at this writing, is seen on cable television.

The charming Cleaver home was and is located at 1727 Buckingham Road in the Wilshire District of Los Angeles. It is a short distance from a home seen in a 1927 Laurel and Hardy classic comedy. Please refer to page 316. The exact façade of the 1727 Buckingham Road house was constructed on the back lot of the production company and can be easily confused with the original (real) structure.

This location is north of the Santa Monica Freeway (10).

*Thomas Brothers Map reference: page 43 at C4. **1992 revised edition**: page 633 at E5.*

Beaver's home. 1727 Buckingham Road, Los Angeles.

Love 'Em and Weep (1927)

One of those magnificent old mansions utilized by Hal Roach to film the immortal comedy team of Laurel and Hardy in one of their zany situations still exists, and hasn't been demolished by the wrecker's ball as so many Laurel and Hardy faithful had thought. It stands today, virtually unchanged from the time of the filming in 1927 (the stone porch railing has been replaced by a wrought iron railing) at the southwest corner of Wellington Road and St. Charles Place in the Wilshire District of Los Angeles. The address is 1705 Wellington Road.

As a bit of trivia, Laurel and Hardy did not receive top billing in this silent film (their fifth). The "star" was Mae Busch. The plot, reworked for their 1931 sound film *Chickens Come Home*, centers on a businessman (James Finlayson) who is visited by an ex-girlfriend (Busch) who produces an old photograph of the two and threatens blackmail. Stanley Laurel, Finlayson's business partner (who is married, as is Finlayson), does Finlayson a favor by keeping Busch occupied while Finlayson co-hosts a dinner at his home.

Laurel picks Busch up at her apartment near downtown Los Angeles. The building, still standing, is located at 610 S. Kenmore Avenue and not at 610 S. Catalina Street as reported in other publications. He takes her to the Pink Pup Cafe (a night club) where she has a bit too much to drink and insists that he drive her to Finlayson's house. Laurel tries to prevent this, but can't as Busch runs to his car and jumps in behind the steering wheel. Laurel becomes a passenger in his own car as Busch drives away. She speeds east on St. Charles Place and skids to a stop in front of Finlayson's house on Wellington Road. Laurel immediately opens the passenger door and falls onto the sidewalk, still attempting to keep Busch from seeing Finlayson. The two struggle all the way up the winding pathway to the entrance of the house.

Inside, Finlayson quickly introduces Busch to his wife as Laurel's wife, then to Oliver Hardy (who finally appears in the film as a party guest) and his wife. The usual sight gags continue inside the house.

At this time a neighborhood busybody who saw Laurel exit the Pink Pup Cafe with Busch, and who followed the two to Finlayson's house in a cab, tells Laurel's wife (Vivien Oakland) of the "affair." A jealous Oakland then grabs a cab and heads for Finlayson's house and arrives just as Finlayson and Laurel are helping Busch out of the front door. Seeing this, Oakland starts a free-for-all in front of the house, involving Laurel, Finlayson and his wife and Hardy and his wife. This melee lasts into the film's closing credits.

The southwest corner of the intersection of Wellington Road and St. Charles Place, the sidewalk, the pathway leading to the entrance to the mansion and the mansion's entrance are seen prominently throughout the latter part of the film and look virtually the same today as in the 1927 film. The mansion is a short distance from the Cleaver home seen in the *Leave It to Beaver* television series.

All locations are north of the Santa Monica Freeway (10).

Thomas Brothers Map reference: page 43 at C4 (the mansion). 1992 revised edition: page 633 at E5; page 43 at F2 (the apartment); 1992 revised edition: page 633 at J2.

The Wellington Road house, a primary location seen in Laurel and Hardy's *Love 'Em and Weep*. (Photo taken in 1989.)

The Kenmore Avenue apartment building where Laurel met Mae Busch in *Love 'Em and Weep*. (Photo taken in 1989.)

Miracle Mile (1989)

To say that this film is a large-scale disaster epic would be putting it mildly. The film centers on the world famous stretch of Wilshire Boulevard from Fairfax Avenue east to Sycamore Avenue, where Johnie's Fat Boy Coffee Shop Restaurant on the northwest corner of the intersection of Fairfax Avenue and Wilshire Boulevard is ground zero for a nuclear attack. The bad guys, of course, are the Russians.

The story revolves around a musician who happens to answer a ringing pay telephone outside Johnie's and learns that the superpowers have launched nuclear missiles and that he is standing on ground zero. Well, the man has but an hour to compete with the 8.5 million persons in Los Angeles County to get out of Los Angeles County.

Thankfully, Johnie's was not really ground zero as the attack was only in the mind of a screenwriter; it stands today in the same old place directly across from the May Co. Department Store.

This location is north of the Santa Monica Freeway (10).

*Thomas Brothers Map reference: page 42 at F2. **1992 revised edition:** page 633 at B2.*

Johnie's Restaurant, the Wilshire Boulevard site of "ground zero" in *Miracle Mile*. (Photo taken in 1989.)

Historic Hollywood
Motion Picture Studios

Charlie Chaplin Studios

Billed as the "first complete motion picture studio in Hollywood" when opened in 1919, this studio complex soon became world famous for producing countless Charlie Chaplin comedies that thrilled moviegoers in virtually every nation.

The most popular feature films produced here were: *The Gold Rush* (1925), *City Lights* (1931), *Modern Times* (1936) and *The Great Dictator* (1940), a 126-minute satire that featured Chaplin in a dual role, one as a Jewish barber in the small country of Tomania, the other as the barber's exact double, Hynkel, the dictator of the country who bore a striking similarity to Adolf Hitler.

This studio is #58 in the city's Historical Cultural Monument listing.

The address is 1416 N. La Brea which is south of Hollywood Boulevard and south of the Hollywood Freeway (101) in Hollywood.

Thomas Brothers Map reference: page 34 at B3. 1992 revised edition: page 593 at D5.

The North La Brea entrance to the Charlie Chaplin Studios. (Photo taken in 1988.)

Columbia Pictures Entertainment Studios

Completed in 1919, the Thomas H. Ince Studios boasted a very beautiful administration building that quickly became a Culver City landmark. Many motion picture and television production companies owned the studio complex in later years, including RKO, Pathé, Desilu and Grant Tinker/Gannett.

The administration building is instantly recognized by motion picture fans as it was the "mansion" seen in the opening credits of many Selznick International Pictures productions, the most famous being the 1939 epic *Gone with the Wind.*

The Washington Boulevard entrance to the administration building is world famous as the entrance with the long walkway leading to the Atlanta, Georgia, mansion Rhett Butler (Clark Gable) built for his new wife, Scarlett (Vivien Leigh). This location is first seen in this film classic when three of Scarlett's servants, Mammy (Hattie McDaniel), Pork (Oscar Polk), and Prissy (Butterfly McQueen), approach, baggage in hand, and are awestruck at the mansion's beauty. The trio then enter the grounds from Washington Boulevard and go slowly toward the entrance.

This Atlanta mansion, however, is not the Selznick Studios administration building. It is merely a painting on glass, a trick shot (special effect) by Hollywood's special effects wizard, Jack Cosgrove, who received an Academy Award nomination for his efforts.

As a note of interest, a local historical society claims that the studio's back lot was torched for the famous burning of Atlanta scenes of *Gone with the Wind.* A few years ago, however, a spokesperson for the old MGM Studios (now Sony Pictures) a short distance away claimed that this filming took place on the back lot of MGM Studios which is now a residential area of Culver City, immediately west of the present studio complex.

The Sony Corporation recently purchased this piece of Hollywood motion picture history to house its Columbia Pictures television operations, *Gone with the Wind* history notwithstanding.

The studio complex is located at 9336 W. Washington Boulevard, at the intersection of Ince Boulevard, south of the Santa Monica Freeway (10).

Thomas Brothers Map reference: page 42 at C6. 1992 revised edition: page 672 at H1.

Top: The Washington Boulevard entrance to the administration building of Columbia Pictures seen in the opening credits of Selznick International Pictures features and as the entrance leading to Rhett and Scarlett's Atlanta, Georgia, mansion in *Gone with the Wind*. (Photo taken in 1988.) *Bottom:* A closer view of the walkway as seen in *Gone with the Wind*. (Photo taken in 1986.)

Walt Disney Studio (Site)

The first formal Walt Disney Studio opened in Los Angeles in 1926. Many outstanding animated cartoons and features of the 1920s, 1930s and 1940s were filmed there; *Snow White and the Seven Dwarfs* (1937) was the most memorable.

The studio complex *was* located at 2719 Hyperion Avenue. No sign of the studio exists today. A supermarket now occupies the area. Its address is 2725 Hyperion Avenue, east of Los Feliz Boulevard and west of the Golden State Freeway (5).

Walt Disney and his brother, Roy, moved their massive production company to more spacious quarters in the city of Burbank. The address is 500 South Buena Vista Street, north of the Ventura Freeway (134).

The site of the first formal Walt Disney Studio is #163 in the city of Los Angeles' Historical Cultural Monument listing.

Thomas Brothers Map reference: page 35 at B2 (original site). 1992 revised edition: page 594 at C3; page 24 at C3 (present site); 1992 revised edition: page 563 at F3.

A supermarket now on the site of the old Walt Disney Studio. (Photo taken in 1986.)

Metro-Goldwyn-Mayer Studios (Sony Corporation)

This famous motion picture institution began producing feature films in 1924. The studio facilities expanded rapidly to eventually encompass 117 acres of Culver City real estate.

There are several entrances into the studio complex. Only two, however, are familiar to moviegoers: the "classic" entrance on Washington Boulevard west of Madison Avenue and the so-called "deco" entrance at the end of Grant Avenue, west of Madison Avenue. These entrances were used in many motion picture trailers to promote various features produced by the studio over the decades.

The studio complex, much smaller today, has changed owners several times of late and is now owned by the Sony Corporation.

The studio's address is 10202 W. Washington Boulevard. This location is south of the Santa Monica Freeway (10).

Thomas Brothers Map reference: page 42 at C6. 1992 revised edition: page 672 at G1.

The "classic" entrance to the old MGM Studios on Washington Boulevard. (Photo taken in 1986.)

The "deco" entrance to the old MGM Studios on Grant Avenue. (Photo taken in 1988.)

Monogram Studios (KCET Television Studios)

This motion picture production company was one of the Big Three of Poverty Row along with Republic Studios and PRC (Producers Releasing Corporation).

Republic Studios, without question, had the best product of the three, closely followed by PRC—which leaves Monogram at the bottom of the barrel.

But Monogram did sustain the neighborhood movie houses during the Golden Days of Hollywood by producing over 700 feature films, the most popular being the Bowery Boys and Charlie Chan series.

In earlier decades, film legends Charlie Chaplin, Fatty Arbuckle and the Keystone Kops all made movies at this studio. The studio was also the site of the opening scenes of the film classic *Invasion of the Body Snatchers* (1956). Please refer to that section of this book for further information.

The studio is #198 in the city's Historical Cultural Monument listing.

The old studio is located behind a television studio (KCET Television, Channel 28) at 4401 Sunset Boulevard, east of Vermont Avenue and north of the Hollywood Freeway (101) in Los Angeles.

Thomas Brothers Map reference: page 35 at A3. 1992 revised edition: page 594 at B4.

The Sunset Boulevard entrance to the old Monogram Studios (now KCET Television Studios). (Photo taken in 1988.)

Paramount Studios

In a clever bit of worldwide advertising, Paramount Pictures executives arranged for many of their motion pictures to be filmed at or near the studio entrance, making the entrance and the Paramount logo familiar to moviegoers in virtually every nation in the world. Scenes from the classic *Sunset Boulevard* (1950), *Hollywood or Bust* (1956) which proved to be the last team appearance of Dean Martin and Jerry Lewis, and the Jerry Lewis comedy *The Errand Boy* (1961) are prime examples.

A much larger entrance to the studio complex was constructed west of the now famous "classic" entrance. And even though the new entrance retains the basic architecture of the original entrance, the original studio entrance remains an attraction to thousands of tourists annually.

The new main entrance to the studio is located at 5555 Melrose Avenue. The "classic" entrance is a short distance east, north of the intersection of Melrose Avenue and Bronson Avenue, at the end of Bronson Avenue.

*Thomas Brothers Map reference: page 34 at D5. **1992 revised edition:** page 593 at G6.*

The "classic" entrance to Paramount Studios at the end of Bronson Avenue, north of Melrose Avenue. (Photo taken in 1988.)

Sennett Studios

Built by motion picture pioneer Mack Sennett in 1912, the original studio complex was one of the first motion picture studios in Los Angeles.

This solitary reminder of the beginning of Hollywood motion pictures rests on a slope east of Glendale Boulevard at the intersection of Effie Street.

Once a part of Sennett's "Fun Factory," this building now houses a theater group's scenery and wardrobe. In years past it served as a roller skating rink and as a Western dance hall.

The studio is #256 in the city's Historical Cultural Monument listing.

The address is 1712 Glendale Boulevard, north of the Hollywood Freeway (101).

Thomas Brothers Map reference: page 35 at C5. 1992 revised edition: page 594 at E6.

The last building of the Sennett Studios on the east side of Glendale Boulevard at the intersection of Effie Street. (Photo taken in 1986.)

The south entrance to the "Fun Factory." (Photo taken in 1986.)

Historic Movie Ranches

Arnaz Ranch (Site)

The Arnaz Ranch, once a part of the vast Jose De Arnaz Spanish land grant in the Rincon De Los Bueyes section of the city of Los Angeles, was a spacious area with rolling hills and groves of eucalyptus trees not far from Culver City. This rural setting attracted the attention of motion picture producer Hal Roach who purchased the property.

Segments of many Hal Roach films were shot on the ranch, including scenes of Laurel and Hardy's *Towed in a Hole* (1932) and Our Gang's *School's Out* (1930), *The Pooch* (1932) and *Helping Grandma* that was released the month, day and year I was born, January 3, 1931.

The ranch site (now a housing tract) is located west of Robertson Boulevard, between David Avenue and Beverlywood Street, north of the Santa Monica Freeway (10).

*Thomas Brothers Map reference: page 42 at D4. **1992 revised edition: page 632 at H6.***

In the heart of the old Arnaz Ranch, on David Avenue looking east toward Robertson Boulevard. (Photo taken in 1988.)

Iverson Ranch

The rugged landscape of this historic motion picture location some 30 miles from downtown Los Angeles was the setting for more than 2,000 motion pictures and movie serials from the 1930s through the 1950s. Virtually every boulder, stagecoach trail, gorge, railroad tunnel and twisting highway both on the ranch property and in the immediate area has been filmed countless times for a myriad of motion pictures as well as for scores of television series productions.

Indian Head Rock is perhaps the most familiar of the many rock formations scattered about the ranch property. It was seen in *The Amazonians* and *David and Goliath* as early as 1920. It was later seen in *Tell It to the Marines* (1925), and in *Noah's Ark* (1928) as the spot on the top of Mount Ararat, the 16,946 foot mountain where the Biblical ark supposedly settled after the Great Flood began to recede. In the classic movie serial *The Phantom Empire* (1935) it was seen as a part of Radio Ranch, Gene Autry's ranch on the earth's surface, high above the underground kingdom of Murania that was located 20,000 feet below.

Errol Flynn's *The Charge of the Light Brigade* (1936), Laurel and Hardy's *The Flying Deuces* (1939), John Wayne's *Stagecoach* (1939) and *The Fighting Seabees* (1944), Roy Roger's *Frontier Pony Express* (1939), Henry Fonda's *The Grapes of Wrath* (1940), Bill Elliott's *Wagon Wheels Westward* (1945) and Gene Autry's *The Hills of Utah* (1951) are a few of the many motion pictures filmed in areas across the ranch property.

Of interest to Laurel and Hardy fans, the segment of *The Flying Deuces* filmed at the ranch turned out to be the famous laundry scene wherein Stan Laurel and Oliver Hardy as French Foreign Legionnaires assigned to laundry duty as punishment, quickly tire of washing and ironing tons of white clothing and stomp off the job to tell the Commandant (Charles Middleton) they have decided to resign. In their haste they accidentally overturn a stove and set the laundry afire. Please refer to *The Flying Deuces* section of this book for further information.

Many motion picture serials were filmed at this location, including Gene Autry's *The Phantom Empire*, mentioned earlier, *Terry and the Pirates* (1940), *Dick Tracy Vs. Crime, Inc.* (1941) and *The Adventures of Captain Marvel* (1941) that starred my good friend Frank Coghlan, Jr., as Billy Batson who suddenly became Captain Marvel (Tom Tyler) when he shouted *Shazam!*

Segments of television's *The Big Valley, Gunsmoke, Have Gun—Will Travel, The Lone Ranger, The Rifleman* and *Wagon Train* were also filmed here.

Of late, however, "progress" has taken its toll as much of the area is now under development with condos replacing the cowboys, horses and covered wagons of the Old West.

Concerned, I contacted the contractor. A spokesperson assured me that the basic landscape of the ranch as well as the rock formations will be left intact as much as possible for historic reasons, thus allowing the visitor to enjoy this important piece of motion picture history by either driving the roads or walking the paths and sidewalks to a familiar motion picture film location.

The main entrance to the ranch leads to "California West, a Private Residential Community." En route, look to the right. The famous Lone Ranger Rock can be seen as well as the Lone Ranger Trail (to the right and below the rock), both of which appeared in the opening segment of each program.

To relive the history of Iverson Ranch in words and photographs, I urge you to obtain a copy of Robert G. Sherman's "Quiet on the Set!" as it is an outstanding revelation of motion pictures filmed at this location over the decades.

Iverson Ranch is now bisected by the Simi Valley Freeway (118), west of the Golden State Freeway (5).

To reach the ranch, go west on the Simi Valley Freeway from the Golden State Freeway. Exit at Topanga Canyon Boulevard. Turn left (south) and go a short distance down Topanga Canyon Boulevard to the first intersection, Santa Susana Pass Road. Turn right (west) and go approximately 1 mile up this twisting road to the ranch entrance.

Thomas Brothers Map reference: page 6 at B1. 1992 revised edition: page 499 at J2.

The famous Lone Ranger Rock near the entrance to the ranch. Both rock and the nearby trail were seen in the opening segment of each *Lone Ranger* television episode. (Photo taken in 1989.)

The Lone Ranger Trail. (Photo taken in 1989.)

Top: The famous Indian Head Rock seen in *The Amazonians* (1920), *David and Goliath* (1920), *Tell It to the Marines* (1925) and *The Phantom Empire* (1935). (Photo taken in 1986.) *Bottom:* An opposite view of Indian Head Rock seen in *Noah's Ark* (1928). (Photo taken in 1986.)

Iverson's famous Arch Rock in 1986, a familiar location seen in many Lash La Rue
Westerns and in many episodes of television's *The Lone Ranger.*

Arch Rock in 1989, behind a backyard fence as condos approach.

Iverson Ranch, now occupied with condos. Note the view of the San Fernando Valley in the right center of the photograph. (Photo taken in 1989.)

More condos creeping across the historic ranch. (Photo taken in 1989.)

Melody Ranch

Cowboy legend Gene Autry rode the streets and trails of his "personal" ranch thousands of times over the decades, making the ranch buildings, houses and arched entrance to the ranch familiar to Western motion picture fans worldwide.

Although now surrounded by homes, Melody Ranch, surprisingly, remains intact, looking much as it did during the Golden Era of movie Westerns in the 1930s, 1940s and 1950s.

The ranch is located on Oak Creek Avenue at Placeritos Boulevard, north of Placerita Canyon Road, west of the Antelope Freeway (14) in Newhall.

Thomas Brothers Map reference: page 127 at E3. 1992 revised edition: page 4641 at B1.

The following photographs are of various locations in the Melody Ranch complex seen in scores of Westerns over the decades.

The entrance to Melody Ranch. (Photo taken in 1986.)

An old fort. (Photo taken in 1986.)

The old town hall/church/schoolhouse, etc. (Photo taken in 1986.)

An old locomotive on the "Back 40" of the ranch. (Photo taken in 1986.)

Potpourri for the Film Buff

At times, Hollywood history is evident but can't be seen. Such is the case with the famous prison site from the 1927 Laurel and Hardy classic comedy *The Second Hundred Years.*

The "prison" seen in the film and its gigantic wrought iron gate was, in reality, the old Goodyear Tire and Rubber plant that *was* located on Central Avenue, between Florence Avenue and Gage Avenue in South-Central Los Angeles.

The gate so prominent in the film was located on the east side (Central Avenue) of the once massive facility where 69th Street intersects. It was a magnificent site for many years but, sadly, fell victim to time and progress.

The entire Goodyear facility was demolished and replaced by an enormous post office complex, leaving Laurel and Hardy, the prison, the gate and their famous "paint escape" scene to the film itself and to the memories of those who were fortunate enough to actually see this site in person.

This location is east of the Harbor Freeway (110). *Thomas Brothers Map reference: page 52 at C5. 1992 revised edition: page 674 at E7.*

To compound the "film location hunt," some television production companies are very elusive in relation to revealing some film locations. The house seen in *Married . . . with Children* since the program's opening segment that aired on April 5, 1987, is an example. The storyline places it in Chicago, Illinois. Well, after searching many leads, I finally contacted the production company and was informed that, yes, the house is located in Chicago. I don't believe it but I'll have to accept it.

The Tanner residence seen in *ALF* is another example. Seen during the program since the first telecast on September 22, 1986, this house has proved very difficult to locate, primarily due to the production company's effort to protect the privacy of the family that resides in the house and the neighbors as well. I learned that the house is located in the West Los Angeles area.

I had no such problem a few years ago during a vacation in Mexico. A tour bus stopped on a cliff overlooking a beautiful bay outside the lovely city of Puerto Vallarta. This location was seen in the 1964 Richard Burton film *The Night of the Iguana*. The very gracious guide welcomed questions relating to this film location and encouraged us to take photographs.

A beautiful Puerto Vallarta, Mexico, beach, the primary film location for *The Night of the Iguana* (1964). (Photo taken in 1985.)

INDEX

Numbers in **boldface** refer to pages with photographs.

343